3@

Also by Susan L. Taylor

*In the Spirit: The Inspirational Writings of Susan L. Taylor*
*Lessons in Living*
*Confirmation: The Spiritual Wisdom That Has Shaped Our Lives*
(coauthored with Khephra Burns)


*ESSENCE* Books Under the Creative Direction of
Susan L. Taylor

*ESSENCE: 25 Years Celebrating Black Women*
*50 of the Most Inspiring African-Americans*
*Beauty Basics & Beyond: 101 Ways to Keep Your Hair & Skin Fabulous*
*Making It Happen: Creating Success and Abundance*
*Black Men: In Their Own Words*
*21st Century Sister: The ESSENCE Five Keys to Success*
*ESSENCE Total Makeover: Body, Beauty, Spirit*

# ALL ABOUT *Love*

Favorite Selections From
## *In the Spirit*
on Living Fearlessly

## By Susan L. Taylor

URBAN BOOKS

Urban Books
1199 Straight Path
West Babylon, NY 11704

ISBN-13: 978-1-60162-114-6
ISBN-10: 1-60162-114-0

First Printing February 2008
10   9   8   7   6

Printed in the United States
of America

Submit Wholesale Orders to:
Kensington Publishing Corp.
c/o Penguin Group (USA) Inc.
Attention: Order Processing
405 Murray Hill Parkway
East Rutherford, NJ 07073-2316
Phone: 1-800-526-0275
Fax: 1-800-227-9604

For  mina Suzanne King

For the children who are suffering anywhere;
that their needs will become our compass.

# acknowledgments

Much of what is in this volume I have learned from the many original thinkers whose teachings have had a profound influence on my understanding and vision. I am deeply grateful to them.

I thank my gifted friends and colleagues for helping me expand my writing and for rewriting and polishing my work: A. J. Verdelle, Rosemarie Robotham, Michael Eric Dyson, asha bandele and Lena Sherrod. asha and Lena circled me with love and wise witness and pushed me to finish this book.

I thank the designers of the book, my most generous and talented colleague for the past twenty years, LaVon Leak-Wilks, and Pinda Diarrassouba-Romain; my gentle and strong literary agent, Marie Brown; my skillful copy editor, Gil Griffin; and my devoted assistant Debra Parker for her loyalty and excellent work.

I am grateful to Terrie Williams, Rev. Andriette Earl, Trish Ramsay, Pat Martin, Peggy Ruffin, and Roxanna Bilal, beloved womenfriends who give me the courage to dream, risk and heal.

My deepest gratitude to the man of my dreams, my husband, Khephra Burns, for his penetrating eye, piercing analysis, tenderness and love.

# on a personal note

I have polished and expanded some of the writings here, which are among
my favorites, as well as the favorites of many *Essence* readers over the years.
Several themes reoccur in this volume—finding harmony with ourselves
and others; shedding the old skin of anger and bitterness, opening the heart
and soul fully to love; wealth building and abundance; commitment to
personal and social change; strengthening our families and communities; and,
primarily, keeping faith and finding the face of God in all our challenges.
These are the principles and values that embody the wisdom I'm trying to
live each day.

In keeping with your personal needs and taste, you may want to read the
essays in the categories in which they are grouped, or simply let the book open
on any page. However you come to these offerings, I hope they will speak to
your heart.

# contents

## 1
### Introduction
A Bridge of Light

## 13
### Being Peace

## 45
### Paths to God

# contents

# contents

# contents

# contents

# contents

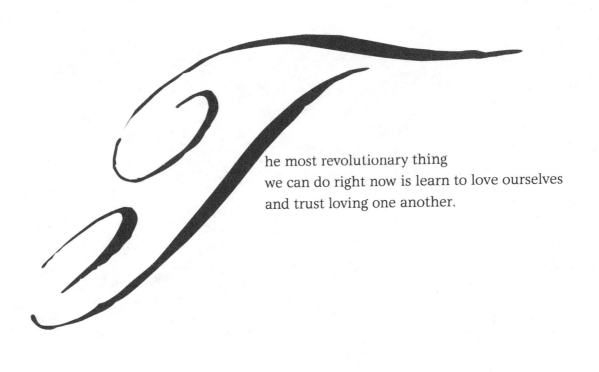

The most revolutionary thing
we can do right now is learn to love ourselves
and trust loving one another.

# A Bridge of Light

For more than two and a half decades, In the Spirit, my monthly column in *Essence* magazine, has been something of a public diary. In those pages I've shared my hopes, dreams and passions and untangled the fears that sometimes took hold of me and caused me to do battle with myself. Along the way, I've learned that there is nothing in the world that stunts our lives like fear—and nothing that nourishes our spirit like love.

As a child, I feared that my parents didn't love me enough. My father's stern silence and my mother's constant criticism would hurt my heart. As a young professional, I feared that my tender heart would be viewed as weakness in the workplace, where the destructive use of power is often equated with success. In my relationships, I feared saying yes and feared saying no; I was fearful of losing as well as of winning. When a close friend betrayed me, I shut down and became untrusting, refusing to reveal myself even though I was desperately lonely and longing for love and connection. Fear is lethal. It kills hope and happiness, makes us its plaything. And like a fungus, it flourishes in the dark.

Writing In the Spirit has been my bridge of light. Examining each month the difficult issues we wrestle with has been clarifying and healing. Over time, I have written about personal events I thought I would never dare to share—none more painful than being thrown onto my own as a young single mother. My heart still aches when I remember that time. My first marriage crumbled when my daughter, Shana, was a newborn, just six weeks old. I was five months pregnant when I discovered Billy was seeing "Pam," the cute sister who worked for him in his Harlem beauty salon. Eventually he just stopped coming home, and there was nothing I could do about it. I hurt so badly some days it was difficult to breathe.

By that time Daddy had died and Mommy had her own financial and emotional woes, and I didn't want to put another burden on my Babs. I was swamped with feelings of betrayal, sadness and jealousy, and I was also mad as hell. Having a baby wasn't my idea, it was Billy's. And now he was gone. I hid my anguish from my family, but it was during this crisis that I learned to value deeply my faithful womenfriends. How strengthening it is when you know sisters love you and have your back! My girl Peggy Ruffin had grown up in the Johnson housing projects just around the corner from me in East Harlem. She stood strong by my side all through my pregnancy. Every day Peggy checked in with me. She'd come by to visit, invite me out to dinner, cook for me. Lord knows she tried to pull me out of my misery. And though my beloved Trish Ramsay had already moved back home to Jamaica, when my life seemed to be unraveling, her arms reached across the waters and held me tight. Trish's encouraging letters and affirming phone calls were a constant.

There are no gifts greater than compassion and kindness in time of need—my Peg-Legs and Trishy taught me that. I also learned that everyone in our life plays a part in our development. Billy, too. He taught me that nothing is forever, that I was stronger than I knew; and ultimately I discovered the power in surrendering hurt and bitterness to forgiveness and gratitude. The end of our marriage also showed me that a woman must always have money of her own and should think long and hard before choosing to become a mother.

These are some of the lessons I have written about over the years in In the Spirit. The column became as much about sharing my thoughts and struggles with our readers as it was about bearing witness to my own emergence. And in time, In the Spirit grew to be our private discussion, at once a knowing whisper between sisters—and brothers too—and a gentle reminder that we are always securely in God's care.

It's amazing. Today, Billy and I are cool. We have love for each other and realize that we gave each other the best we had at the time: Our daughter, Shana was our great gift. But perhaps the most profound insight I gained from our partnership is this: Hurt people hurt people. People who inflict pain on others have been deeply hurt themselves. Billy brought to our marriage deep, unresolved pain from his childhood in Virginia. And I brought my wounds to the union as well. But God was always in attendance. What I thought was an unbearable tragedy turned out to be the transformation that set me on a path to happiness and fulfillment.

Our greatest challenge at each moment is to let go of the burdens of the past. We can release our heavy baggage. It's so important that we find safe harbor, open up and tell our truths so that we will no longer be ruled by our sorrows, but will come to understand how those experiences can lead us to self-knowledge and powerful transformation.

## The Masks We Wear

The reflections collected in this volume are those that have been most meaningful to *Essence* readers and to me. As I travel within and outside the United States, women and men approach me to talk about the In the Spirit columns that have spoken to them the most. Along with the correspondence I receive, these personal conversations have become vital to my work. At times they've created a deep urge to run home and write. Never having thought of myself as a teacher, but as a wisdom seeker trying to lift myself above my own insecurities and fears, I have found it astonishing to hear from so many that my writings and talks have helped them transform their lives. Over the years many have suggested that I collect in one volume the columns that have been most meaningful to them—and to me. This book is evidence that I have listened.

Writing In the Spirit led me to many wise souls and books of wisdom. Each helped reshape my consciousness, leading me to the supreme discovery that I might not otherwise have discerned in our angst-ridden world: Love is always the answer. Put your faith and trust in God, Allah, Jehovah, Yahweh, Shiva, the Lord, the One—whatever you may call love. Bathe every cell of your being in God's divine love, and everything that's not nourishing and godlike in your life will fall away.

With faith and a committed belief, nothing is impossible. Faith keeps us connected to God's power and also to our history and the loving hearts of our ancestors. Love is our protection, more powerful than anything that walks on earth. This is the truth our soul already knows. It is what our brother Jesus came here to teach us. Love and faith—the unseen forces in life—open doors to miracles.

In the Spirit is about facing our fears and feeding our faith. I write about what we're all longing for on this journey—peace, self-acceptance, a deeper connection to God and one another, more love. In the Spirit is about the baby steps we can take to get there. Having spoken and listened to so many of you over the years in cities throughout the nation, the Motherland and the Diaspora, I learned that, like me, many people were raised with the idea that who they are is unacceptable. But we are here. We made it through, praise God! Yet we cannot forget that so many of us got lost along the way.

Even for those of us still standing, society's rules pull us away from ourselves, from who we are, from what's unique about us, what needs to be heard, witnessed, validated and honored. No wonder so many of us wear a mask in order to navigate our world and try to fit in. We learn to protect ourselves, to cover our fear and our fury and bury those parts of ourselves that feel vulnerable to cruelty. We use food, drugs, alcohol, sex, material excess and often bitterness to hide our pain. Our masks are as varied and complex as we are, and each time we put one on, the action costs us pieces of our dignity, our fearlessness, our self-respect.

Forgetting who we are is serious business. It's painful living in a place that's not your home. It's debilitating when your life is an enactment of the expectations of others. And as the need to please others grows greater than your own self-regard, the problems begin: headaches, stomach tied in knots, phobias and neuroses. When we forget who we are, we forfeit our dreams and lose sight of what we came to Earth to do. Our voice becomes a whisper, anger arises, and illness takes root. It's impossible to be focused and feel fulfilled when our heart is broken and we have no peace—all because we have forgotten who we are and feel disconnected from God's love: the mysterious divine source within that is always wise and clear and our home.

My monthly commitment to In the Spirit has been a special blessing for me. Honoring my deadline forces me to make time for stillness and inner listening and to reconnect with my soul. But I didn't come to writing In the Spirit easily. When I first became editor-in-chief of *Essence* in 1981, I'd barely done any writing at all. Our former chief editor, Marcia Ann Gillespie, is a brilliant and prolific writer, and under her guidance I'd written some fashion and beauty copy, but that was it. In fact, when I accepted the editor-in-chief's position, I tried to convince our then-publisher and cofounder, Ed Lewis, that my writing a column wasn't necessary. He said, "No deal. Our readers must hear from you."

I resisted because I was afraid my little offering would be negatively compared with Marcia's amazing editorials. Had I not been forced to step out there, I never would have connected so deeply with myself, with you or with our community. I never would have realized that I wasn't "on the ledge alone," as my dear friend Terrie Williams says. Had I not begun the journey, I may not have come to realize that anxiety and fear are mostly of our own invention.

But frightened as I was, I took the first step, which is all God asks of us. And in that very moment my mask thinned. I began to value the freedom and healing power of telling the truth. When we tell the truth with a loving intention we are expressing faith, which surrounds us with an aura of protection. Our world becomes a safe place. We embody courage and give up the fear of being criticized. Anyone who would stand against you has no more power to hurt you; they are rendered incapable of harming a single hair on your head. *No weapon formed against you shall prosper.*

## Walk-on-Water Faith

It's not always easy to face ourselves and the unwise choices we have made. At times I still resist. But not facing what is hurting doesn't diminish the pain. During slavery—the worst period for us throughout the Diaspora—most of our ancestors never spoke about the wrenching pain of losing loved ones, the repeated rapes, the unspeakable acts of violence and humiliation they withstood. But not speaking of the immeasurable harm and how it left them did not make the wounds less deep or the scars less defining. They are visible today in the hurt we cause ourselves and one another, in the ways we sometimes speak to one another, with tongues as harsh as any overseer's lash. Yes, we are the children of brave survivors, but those survivors did not only pass down to us their courage, they also passed down their pain. We are still in recovery.

I haven't always had the strength to face my own troubles. As a very young woman, I didn't do it at all. I learned how to dampen my pain when I was a girl not feeling the love I so longed for from my stoic and distant West Indian parents. At times I would find myself in dangerous places, in back stairwells in the arms of the boys in my Harlem tenement. And as a young single mother, feeling lonely, lost and hungering for love, I allowed into my home, and at times into my bed, men who should never have been in my life. There was one who loved me so much, but along with his sweetness and support, he also brought drugs—a truth I have just found the courage to reveal. Today I shudder when I think about the unwise choices I made from a place of incompleteness and longing, choices made in secret and silence, putting my beloved daughter, Shana, and our future at risk.

We keep our lives secret because we fear being judged or abandoned or losing love. Here are words of love and wisdom spoken by the late Audre Lorde, one of the world's finest minds and writers, in a speech she delivered to lesbian scholars and included in her courageous book *The Cancer Journals*, which should be read by every woman. Audre, whom I came to know and love, began writing the journal entries six months after having a mastectomy for breast cancer.

*What are the words you do not yet have? What do you need to say?*
*What are the tyrannies you swallow day by day and attempt to make*
*your own, until you will thicken and die of them, still in silence?*
*Perhaps for some of you here today, I am the face of one of your fears.*
*Because I am woman, because I am black, because I am lesbian,*
*because I am myself, a black woman warrior poet doing my work,*
*come to ask you, are you doing yours?*

*And, of course, I am afraid—you can hear it in my voice—because*
*the transformation of silence into the language and action is an act of*
*self-revelation and that always seems fraught with danger. But my*

*daughter, when I told her of our topic and my difficulty with it, said, "Tell them about how you're never really a whole person if you remain silent, because there's always that one little piece inside of you that wants to be spoken out, and if you keep ignoring it, it gets madder and madder and hotter and hotter, and if you don't speak it out one day it will just up and punch you in the mouth."*

I am grateful to have heard those words, so grateful to have survived my ignorance and to have thrived. God is good and I am thankful that I began to notice myself. But still at times I am shaken. Fortunately, those moments are now fewer and further apart. But as is true for every one of us, at times things fall apart: There have been fissures in my family, mad fights behind the scenes at *Essence*, personal losses. Menopause challenged my memory and made me think I was losing my mind. I have had my breath taken away by events in our community—the lack of support for survivors of the Gulf Coast hurricanes; the miseducation and overincarceration of our young. But I've come to believe that even these wrenching realities are part of the grand design.

No matter how difficult the situation, our question must always be—as Rumi, the thirteenth-century mystic and one of my favorite poets, asks: *What has this new arrival, sent by a guide from beyond, come to teach me?*

Whatever is happening to us at this moment is a potential source of wisdom, sent to wake us and remind us that our innate power is equal to every moment. To live life from a place of serenity requires total trust in God—walk-on-water faith and belief in love. It also requires that we not sleepwalk through the tasks at hand. We have to stay awake and have a plan.

## God Is Love

By telling even my most painful stories—Mommy's death, infidelity and violence in relationships, the many mistakes I made mothering solo, my battles with insecurity—I have come to see that loss, pain and sadness are as natural and important to our lives as are the rewards and the times of sheer joy. But somehow we come to adulthood expecting painless deliverance or supernatural intervention, as if someone will swoop in and save us from ourselves and life. We want to say a little prayer, a little affirmation, a mantra, a rosary and be done with it. Problem solved!

It would be wonderful if we could snap our fingers and make everything challenging go away. Who among us wouldn't have chased the storms away with a word, receded the waters in New Orleans with the blink of an eye, let a hand raised up to God make it so no child anywhere ever suffers? But that's not how it goes. We have to have a plan. Have to do the work. Now, here is the good news: For every problem in our lives, there's a solution. We are the most powerful tool we have. In the Spirit helped me understand this. Writing is my walk and way to understanding, love and faith.

Like you, I live in a world spilling over with responsibilities: family, work, caring for myself, trying to keep my love life and my money straight—all while trying to stay aware of what's happening in the world and find ways to do my part to make a difference in the lives of our people. But just as "in our Father's house there are many mansions," there are also worlds within us in which we must reside. Yes, we must keep clear the demanding world of details and deadlines, but we must keep clear another world, our spiritual one. It's there and only there where we can see and touch the divine order at the heart of any upheaval.

Our work in life is to merge the two worlds. We can do it. Must do it. Human beings have made every corner of the planet a disaster zone, and human beings have the power and responsibility to clear and clean it up, set the Earth back on its axis. We are not small or powerless. We have the ability to transform our world. Our personal and collective pain, the disorder all around us, are calls to get up and get moving. So many are suffering greatly, but suffering is for one purpose: to teach us compassion. From the realm of spirit, we all are part of a mass consciousness. Our collective negativity and passivity have made this a very dangerous world. By living right and trusting in the greatest force in the universe—love—we can make our communities safe, productive and loving and give our children the future they deserve.

The point of every single In the Spirit column has been to encourage us to trust life, to renew our faith each moment that the loving and wise spirit of God is within us, surrounding and sustaining us, renewing us, calling forth in us what is better and new. There is nothing I care more about than learning how to trust love, how to find my way home to God. After a childhood during which the love of my parents and a personal relationship with God seemed like distant lands whose borders I could not penetrate, I searched for another way, a path laid with evident signs of tenderness, understanding and love. I wanted to walk that path. What a great blessing it is to share with you what I am learning along the journey.

The writings included here are the works that resonate most with me, the ones that best illuminate how life is always working to support our highest and greatest good. Like you, I want inner peace. I want it for all of us and I want it right now. I want our community restored yesterday and every vulnerable child made whole this day. I want war to end, peace and justice to take its place. I want never to feel uncertain or anxious again. But it's the ego that wants everything to happen on a timeline we create. It's the ego that doesn't know that God is always on time.

I am learning, even now, to dissolve the dualistic tension between me and them, this and that, good and bad. I'm learning more each day to trust the flow of life, to "lean into the sharp points," relaxing into them, inviting them to prick me, and to see what they have come to teach me before they can really wound me, which is what we do to ourselves when we don't listen up, when we ignore the warning signs, those first pricks.

The whole point of my work these past 25 years has been to understand that in order for balance to be achieved in the world around us, it must first be achieved in the world inside us. This volume draws from the breadth of the writings I have shared with millions of people through *Essence*. Though the audience is vast, my relationship with my sisters is a deep, passionate and personal one. Together we have raised children and we have buried parents. We have watched cities drown and we have seen spirits rise up. We have lost some of our babies, but we have also been saved by some. Together we have renegotiated our faith, our relationships, and our way back to ourselves and to God. We have been comforted by, and have given comfort with, love and forgiveness. We have learned that God, by whatever name we call the Divinity—Amma, Allah, Jehovah, Lord—is always the answer. The answer is always love.

# Being Peace

*Don't shut the door on troublesome guests. Welcome them*
*with openness and curiosity, but don't let them live with you.*
*Invite them in and ask what they've come to teach you.*

# invitations to happiness

*This being human is a guest-house./Every morning a new arrival./A joy, a depression, a meanness,/some momentary awareness comes/as an unexpected visitor./Welcome and entertain them all!/Even if they're a crowd of sorrows,/who violently sweep your house/empty of its furniture,/still, treat each guest honorably./He may be clearing you out for some new delight./The dark thought, the shame, the malice,/meet them at the door laughing,/and invite them in./Be grateful for whoever comes,/because each has been sent/as a guide from beyond.* —"The Guest-House" by Jalal al-Din Rumi

Life is full of surprises, and as the thirteenth-century Sufi poet Rumi suggested, you never know who or what will come knocking. Throw the doors to life open wide, he says, to welcome whatever may come and look for the gift it brings—and also to invite what is destructive to leave.

Sometimes we lock the worst guests inside, as a sister I'll call Janine did. Preoccupied with the hurt she felt her husband had caused her, Janine was unable to get on with her life. The brother, whom she had put through school, left her for another woman—and with bills, bad credit and their two children. Traumatic, to be sure. But Janine nursed her pain so devoutly that five years after the breakup she was as unhappy as the day he packed his bags, leaving behind a ghost she refused to release.

As was true for Janine, anything in our world can change in an instant. And it's not just the boldface crises that defeat us. Any unwanted event we mentally replay will cost us our peace. Throughout our lifetime we will know anger, shame, fear, depression—these emotions are traits of our human nature, evidence that we are home to a heart and a conscience. Don't shut the door on those troublesome guests. As Rumi advises, welcome them with openness and curiosity, but don't let them live with you. Though they make you feel uncomfortable and anxious for a time, analyzing your discomfort brings the blessing of information. When discomfort arrives, invite it in and ask what it has come to teach you.

Open wide the door to your feelings; make friends with your emotions. Sit still with them when you feel burdened, and listen to the still soft voice whispering, *Turn to Me in any crisis, no matter how large or small; stop struggling, my beloved, and turn to Me.* Soon the sweet, welcome guest, truth, will arrive.

Open the door to faith. It's the guest you want to host forever. Let it fill your heart. Faith has always been sure shelter for Black women. Faith takes strength, and it makes strength. Believe, and the burden will be lifted. Understanding and comfort will come. You begin to see the bigger picture, and in time the way will be clear and bright again.

*No matter what you may be challenged by,
focus on your blessings, a plan to set things
right, and trust God's unshakable love.*

# just stand

What a gift of love Oprah Winfrey bestowed upon us! In tribute to her cherished mentor and friend, she invited nearly 200 folks on a week's cruise in the Gulf of Mexico and the Caribbean. It wasn't the overblown event the press reported it to be, but rather a loving, spirited celebration of a wise soul's birthday: Maya Angelou was turning 70. We were Sister Maya's band, her rainbow tribe, all God's children representing—humanity on the rolling seas. And the fixings? There's no way to recount the splendor of it all. But far more exquisite than anything money could buy was the kindness and joy on board.

This was the retreat from the world of pressures my soul had yearned for. Sister Maya had said it to me years ago: "Downtime is as important as the time you spend hunkered down doing your work." It's how we gain clarity and a new zest for living, she said. I know this—write about it and speak about it—but the wisdom in her words is difficult for us all to live. Many of the guests on the ship—Coretta Scott King and daughter Yolanda, Quincy Jones, Nick Ashford and Valerie Simpson, Andrew Young, choreographer Bill T. Jones, Oprah's beloved friend Gayle King and a host of other amazing folks—said they couldn't remember when they'd had a whole week off from work. For Dr. Dorothy Height, it had been 32 years.

When was the last time you laid your worries down, kicked back and just had some fun?

During that week on the water, I did stuff that I hadn't done in decades. I played games, danced wildly, swam with the dolphins and felt like a kid again! We get so caught up in working and worrying we forget how to play. Laughing and playing aren't frivolous; our joy is the most undeniable evidence of our faith in God. Levity and joy are what you gain when you renew your faith each day in God's enfolding and protecting love.

That truth was affirmed so powerfully at our moving sunrise service on Easter morning. "Just stand," Bebe Winans sang into the heavens as we coursed through the calm, crystal waters. We had church at sea, all of us in white, waving our arms, singing, crying, testifying. There was passionate preaching and praying between the blue of water and sky.

"Just stand," we would smile and say to one another all week. Now I'm holding fast to those two simple words. No matter what the challenge, you can master it. Ask your inner wisdom for a solution or for a way to see it differently, focus on your blessings, and "just stand."

Water is healing—it's the womb of life, and good for reflection and renewal. At times during the journey I felt the spirit of our ancestors among us. As I thought about the horrors they suffered and survived over the seas and centuries, a note of solemnity would touch my joy. Many of our dinner discussions were about the determination of our foreparents, the challenges in our community today and what we owe for the gift of our lives.

Oprah said it best the evening she spoke of Sister Maya's wisdom and love and how they have strengthened her during her darkest hours. Through tears of gratitude, and enfolded in her beloved Stedman's arms, she said she's simply striving to do God's will, to live each day in alignment with her spiritual values. This is the challenge for you and me, to love and trust living for God, for ourselves and for one another.

The loving-kindness that embraced us on board, along with the beauty and rhythm of the water, helped calm and cool my overheated life. Time for rest and renewal is not a luxury. What God wants for us is that we live in balance, that we come to each day with a reverence for life, that we understand how peace and joy on our journey are the natural results of doing things God's way. Then, from a certainty within, we will get on track. We will do what we've been called here to do. And just stand.

*You grow deeply confident when you focus on your true
and unchanging Self. You silence that unrelenting inner critic
who names and blames, compares and condemns you.*

# fire the judge

Diane is a fabulous sister. She's warm, witty and so smart. She speaks several languages, is a technology wiz, and has an M.B.A. Diane travels the world, lends a helping hand to her family, and volunteers at her church. She's an extraordinary person, and everybody knows it—except Diane. She lives in the vise of self-doubt, where she is her own greatest enemy. Her unrelenting self-criticism has caused her to lose confidence in her gifts and talents and at times even life itself.

I've been there, stepping into the world with a veneer of confidence, looking like a self-possessed woman. But scratch the surface and you'd have found a frightened, insecure girl. At times we all have feelings of inadequacy and inferiority. And it's a burdensome struggle trying to hide and control the emotions that accompany feeling "abnormal," or thinking that you must become somebody else to be your best and at ease in the world. Other people seem so powerful, while you want to keep a low profile and shrink away from the world.

Diane's—and our—bogeyman is our inner critic, the self-punishing attitude we layer over our blessings. Eventually it causes us to lose faith in ourselves, in life, love, our amazing healing ability and God. With an ongoing inner dialogue of self-criticism, we judge ourselves harshly and pick ourselves apart. We may tell no one, but self-bickering makes self-loving impossible.

We were born with an inherent confidence and motivation to appreciate ourselves—hardwired to be unique and to develop as the divine original that God created. As children, we thrilled to the mystery and openness of life. We weren't constricted, like adults, by the need to force-fit ourselves into neat little boxes. We told the truth, said what we felt, asked about what we wanted to know. But the "behavior police" deemed that troublesome because it could expose family secrets and taboo subjects, so we stopped being our authentic selves, stopped bringing our truth to light. It's a conditioning not one of us has escaped.

We all have confidence—until we begin the exhausting lifelong struggle of molding ourselves into a distorted and unattainable ideal, an image of perfection that never lets us rest or feel satisfied. We dedicate ourselves to conformity, acceptability and learning how to please others. This killing of our freedom and joy is the main source of our self-doubt and emotional suffering.

Here's what to do: Fire the judge! Get rid of that unrelenting inner critic who names and blames, measures, compares and condemns. God created us as human and divine, perfectly imperfect in the human realm and a model of perfection in the spiritual realm. Our work here is to integrate our two worlds. To live in peace, we must make friends with the challenges of our human nature. We have to acknowledge our fear, guilt, feelings of inadequacy, selfishness, jealousy and vanity and still love and accept ourselves and see ourselves as valuable, not fundamentally flawed.

Disruptive feelings are the dynamics that exist within all of us. These human emotions arise to serve us. They are sometimes gentle and more often eye-opening reminders to lift the veil of illusion that creates a feeling of separation from our Divine Self and help us realize who we truly are.

Run from these disturbing emotions and they'll chase you down, overpower you and toss you around like a plaything. They'll disrupt your life and make you feel fragile and crazy. Love and accept your human nature and you'll gain the momentum, the clarity and the will to learn what the emotions were sent to teach you. You have to love the fullness of your being, your strengths and your weaknesses. Everything in life has its purpose. Our weak spots are to challenge us to move to a higher level of self-love and achievement, to be more patient and extend greater love to others. How else might God get us to practice compassion? All things, all circumstances come to help us increase our faith, to empower us and move us toward feasting on our divinity.

You may be depressed or in debt, overweight, unemployed or ill. But none of these things is your essence, the truth of who you are. These are all human conditions, manageable and transitory, sent from on high to make us question what the hell's going on with us. When we "don't hear," as my mother would say, life does its work, sending us obstacles we cannot ignore—whatever it takes to shake us up, wake us up and make us choose again.

Whatever qualities you attribute to God—love, peace, perfection, beauty, joy, intelligence, creativity, harmony, powerfulness—are yours as well, you are one with them, they are the Life Force, the unchanging truth of who you are. Get in touch with the Life Force, the larger world that is our home, where we and God are one. We can't be separated from the Life Force, our Source, but we can forget about it, and often do.

We, and Diane, will derive a secure sense of self when we focus on our true and unchanging Self—not our human, transitory self that is always in search of someone to recognize and reinforce its existence. Sometime today, in a quiet place, focus on your greater reality and notice the ease and joy you feel. Hold on to the thought of your greater Self and try to infuse every aspect of your life with it. Remember as you go about the everyday of your life—washing your hair, shopping for food, cleaning your home—that you are in and of

God, and you will begin making the gentle evolution, from being a doubting, self-alienated person to having deep confidence, the core of self-esteem. There are those fortunate few folks who easily accept the imperfections of their human nature. The rest of us have to work at it.

Spirit wills itself to you as much as you will yourself to know Spirit. God needs you to help bring heaven to earth. Human and divine, we are the bridge of light between the two worlds. Getting to know your deepest self isn't so difficult. Distinguish unhealthy feelings and behavior from those that make you uniquely who you are. Look at your unwholesome attitudes and habits, get to know them intimately, but don't believe in them, or you'll build a world around them.

Make it easier on yourself. Fire the judge! With love in your heart and your mind on your Sacred Self, which is pleading with you to remember your holy alliance, more and more you'll feel comfortable in your skin and enjoy being who you are. The focus on love and communion shifts the attention from needing to impress and winning the approval of others, to having peace in your life and being a healing force in the world. You stop watching and fearing you'll mess up, say something stupid or look foolish. And if you do, you'll know you still deserve to be loved tenderly and completely because perfection is impossible on the physical plane. You just take yourself as you come, which is quite good enough.

*Ask God for vision and wisdom that matches the light of your soul and they will be given to you—along with everything else you need to live a joyful and meaningful life.*

# living in the light

It's not any fix we're in that causes us to suffer. Rather, it's the stuff we invent about our situation that creates the struggle. It's not who we think we are but what we think we're not that makes us lose our way. The lies and misperceptions we believe about ourselves, which keep us in turmoil, are so deeply ingrained in our emotional landscape that we've become oblivious to them.

"I can't handle the pain" is a lie. "I'm in pain, want to get over it but don't want to do the work of dealing with it right now" is the truth.

"I can't get my weight and health under control" is a lie. "I've been undisciplined and unwilling to make my well-being my top priority" is the truth.

"I can't slow down or take time for myself because of my pressures and responsibilities" is a lie. "There are 168 hours in a week and I've decided to give them all away to my work and others" is the truth.

The truth is the light. Change "I can't" to "I'm not ready to," and the limited view you have of yourself begins to crumble. Then create a workable plan that will help you shape the events of your life so the events don't shape you.

We wouldn't form a business, club or block association without a mission statement, so we shouldn't plan our lives without a personal one. Over the next few weeks, take quiet time to think about how you want to live now and in the future. Write down and commit to memory core values and principles that will keep you fit and focused if you let them govern and guide your life. Then when the daily dramas threaten to rob you of your serenity and focus, remember what you're choosing for yourself.

Our power to choose is an awesome one, an authority we exercise each waking moment, but not always with conscious awareness. We get accustomed to living in the prison of our past or in a fast-forward mode, worrying about the future, missing the brightness, lightness and newness of this holy moment.

Relax. Who you are and where you are situated are necessary steps to where you are going and who you will be. Trust this. Even perceived negatives are for our enlightenment: Having my heart crushed taught me to love not just with my heart but also with my head, and to appreciate the love and support I now rush home to each night. And rational self-doubt made it easy for me to step away from an acting career I wasn't good at and find my passion to work for the community.

The "negatives" around us—homelessness, hunger, violence, our tax dollars being used to build jails for our young rather than to rebuild schools for them—are ultimately to reawaken us and fuel our determination to put an end to Black paralysis.

Ask God for vision and wisdom that matches the light of your soul and they will be given to you—along with everything else you may need to build a joyful and meaningful life. Remember this truth: You were born to succeed, and there really are no negatives, no mistakes—only lessons on living in the light.

*Every day, do something to simplify your life, and*
*you will be a happier, healthier, kinder person, living in*
*this holy moment and not worrying about the next.*

# simplify your life

Our hectic lives are calling us to learn how to live more simply while achieving what we need and desire. But living simply isn't easy when we're addicted to excess, believing that more and bigger and faster are better. There's no peace in perpetual pursuit—no room to experience the sweetness and joy of living when we're constantly doing. These are some helpful ways of simplifying our overextended lives:

**Know what you value.** Monitor what you give your time and attention to. If you value spiritual growth, family time, building up savings and staying healthy, then the work you choose to do and how you spend your leisure time should support those objectives. Otherwise you may find yourself in the mall when you should be in the gym, or working weekends instead of chilling with your family.

**Prioritize.** Put fewer things on your daily schedule and set up a more realistic time frame for each task. Believing we must do everything now puts us under unnecessary pressure. Don't plan to run an errand during a lunch hour if it's going to take more time than you have. Double the time you believe a task will take, and you'll be less stressed, enjoy the process more, and finish with time to spare.

**Regard every activity as a spiritual experience.** You don't need to be in solitude or in a house of worship to feel God's presence. You feel the presence of the Most High the moment you remember that the Holy Spirit is the breath of life in you. Simply remembering to breathe deeply and rhythmically as we go about our day keeps us God-conscious.

In the larger view, each activity is a spiritual experience: attending a meeting, taking care of children, studying, cooking, helping an elder. Each moment is an opportunity to practice the virtues of patience, kindness, forgiveness and, above all, love; they are essential to our spiritual development.

**Separate yourself from negative people and unhealthy relationships.** Choose to be with people who believe in you and encourage you to grow. Stay away from anyone who tears you down or always brings you the latest bad news. If you've tried unsuccessfully to fix a problem marriage or relationship that's making you miserable, it's time to plan your exit. If you need help making the break, get counseling. There are all sorts of services—many of them free—to support women in their choice to move to a better place. Some of the work we have to do is hard and emotionally wrenching, but much of it can be done with another's loving hand on our shoulder.

**Clear the clutter.** Take time over the next month to clean out your closets, handbags, drawers, kitchen cabinets, your desk, your car. Joyfully give away or sell the things you've been hoarding or never use. Take a few minutes before buying anything new and ask yourself if it's something you really need.

**Reduce your expenses.** Few things create more stress than having bills we can't pay. Shop during sales or at consignment shops, buy household items in bulk, schedule long-distance calls for off-hours, eliminate call-waiting. Create and stick to a plan to pay off your bills. And you might try adopting this rule for everything except your home and car: If you can't pay cash for it, pass on it!

God didn't give us the gift of free will so that we would end up having a frenzied, pressured existence. When we simplify our lives we become one with time; we see clearly which activities we should eliminate, how to do things more efficiently and what can be handled by others. And we don't take on a task until we see how it serves God or our highest purpose.

Every day, do something to simplify your life, and you will be a happier, healthier, kinder person, living in this holy moment and not worrying about the next.

*There are detours and service roads but no wrong turns
in life. And it's never too late to take another path.
Ultimately, all things work together for our good.*

# truth or consequences

I remember, as if it were yesterday, sitting in the Cosmo Theater in my East Harlem neighborhood, a star-struck eight-year-old captivated by the self-possessed brown-skinned goddess striding across the screen: Dorothy Dandridge, whose beauty, boldness and sassiness enthralled me. A decade later, when pressed to choose a career—without considering my own interests and talents—I declared I was going to be an actress.

From day one, I was in over my head. Choosing to study with veteran teachers, I found myself in classes with skilled actors, none more phenomenal than those studying with master Lloyd Richards at the Negro Ensemble Company in New York City's East Village. There was Sherman Hemsley, Mary Alice, Marcella Lowery. They were dedicated, passionate and prepared. Most were method actors; they'd burn the midnight oil studying acting techniques, deconstructing characters and learning lines. I got work but never enjoyed it. I played Miss Barkley, the nurse on the CBS soap opera *As the World Turns*, and Minnie, a model, in the film *John and Mary*, starring Mia Farrow and Dustin Hoffman. I was always downright nervous, not fabulous in any role. But lessons keep showing up in our lives, and when we don't learn them easily, they get harder.

I learned a hard lesson when I got a coveted role understudying a female lead in *The Dozens*—a three-character Broadway comedy starring master actors Morgan Freeman, Al Freeman, Jr., and Paula Kelly. Paula, who was onstage for the entire play, was dazzling. Watching her work wonders during the many weeks in that cold rehearsal theater on 42nd Street, I died a slow death. No matter how I tried, I couldn't memorize the lines that Paula seemed to toss about so easily.

What if she caught a cold or needed a day off? And this wasn't a little theater in The Bronx, it was Broadway, and I was terrified. I still get queasy thinking about it.

Waiting nervously in the wings, I never learned the lines, but I did learn this powerful lesson: I should follow my passion, not someone else's. I swore that if I could avoid humiliating myself and creating financial disaster for the producers, I'd be done with acting.

I felt sad for the talented team when the play closed on opening night, but was too thrilled for me. The next day I enrolled in cosmetology school. After graduation, I created a line of natural cosmetics and skin-care products and opened a salon to market them. Nequai Cosmetics, the company bearing my daughter's middle name, led me to *Essence*.

There are detours and service roads but no wrong turns in life. And it's never too late to take another path. Ultimately, all things work together for our good. Agony is God's way of saying, "Change up! This is not what you were sent here to be or do." Act on your truth, or suffer the consequences.

How a thing feels in our soul matters. We must want to pour our whole heart into what we do. Living a lie is much more difficult than building on our dreams: It ties our tongue and our stomach in knots, causes anxiety, illness, all sorts of addictions.

To know what you should be doing, be aware of what's going on within and around you. Are you doing what you love—acting, writing, building a business, revitalizing communities, healing, teaching, practicing law? Are you happy where you spend your days? Do you vibe with the people you work with? Are you proud of what you are creating? What would you do if money and security weren't issues?

The map of your life is within you; go there to find the way. This powerful visualization will help you welcome change and move forward in faith: See yourself joyful, laughing, running toward yourself, your arms flung wide, the wind at your back. Know that wherever you are, you are always in God's embrace, soaring toward your destiny, on your way home.

*Khephra is such a good man. In our many years of marriage, he has never made me cry. Yet I stood ready to rush across the threshold and shake loose drama in my happy home.*

# the way to peace

I'd been standing in my kitchen, fuming. But thank God for second thoughts, for hesitations.

I disagreed with the way my husband, Khephra, was handling a business matter, and I was going to tell him so. Jaw clenched, blood beating in my temples, I marched down the hall to Khephra's office, ready to mess with my heaven. In that moment, God-consciousness was the furthest thing from my mind. But, thankfully, Saving Grace is always near. Hand poised to push open the door, I suddenly stopped cold.

What was I getting ready to do to the best man I know, who since 1989 has always been a good husband, who has brought no pain, no turmoil to our household, who has supported my crazy-busy life and never once complained about my pickiness and peculiarities? Khephra has never made me cry. Yet I stood ready to judge and blame, to rush across the threshold and shake loose drama in our happy home. I wanted to butt in, with no consideration of Khephra's choices, his work, his process, his space. Oh, the flag of ego! It waves red and rants, "Do it my way."

Awareness helps us drop the rant of the ego, which is always looking for offenses, measuring them, rearranging the details to make us feel justified. But things don't have to go our way for us to be happy. We can be happy simply because people we love are happy. I was reminded of this that day when I was ready to pick a fight: Minding my own business is what I should be attending to. Taking care of our own business boosts self-esteem and success, health and happiness. Making others wrong creates disturbance, causes suffering, separation and disharmony in our relationships. This is the root of the carnage in our communities and of the crises in our world.

No two people experience life in exactly the same way, and we can never control another's thoughts or deeds. The forces of apartheid in South Africa controlled the location of Nelson Mandela's body for twenty-seven years, but they could not control his mind, which is why he was able to emerge from his exile ready to inspire and lead. Under pressure beyond our knowing, Mandela kept control of his thoughts because he kept faith and counsel with his God, trusting Spirit's divine design to see him through.

We have to practice letting go of the illusion that we must control every experience. We can start with the little things. Next time someone wants to see a movie that's not our choice or vacation somewhere we didn't choose, let's just go and enjoy ourselves. When our preferences become demands, we put ourselves at odds with life, swimming against the flow, upstream.

As I stood in that hallway outside Khephra's office, I realized that I did not want the negative consequences of what I was about to do. When I visited the great spiritual leader Alice Coltrane at her ashram just months before she left this earth, she told me, "In treating another kindly and lovingly, we are serving humanity, and in serving humanity, we are serving God."

Standing at Khephra's door, I quietly made the choice to serve God instead of bowing to my ego. I took a deep breath, turned around, and folded up my red flag, reaching for acceptance of Khephra, just as he is.

*When you're on a mission of value, God gives you a special blessing. You are divinely guided. You're surrounded at the highest spiritual level with an aura of protection that disarms any enemy and attracts all you need to succeed.*

# mission possible

The stress level for Black people rises high in our world of work. For too many of us—no matter how talented, educated or far along in our careers—the workplace is a painful place. So many of us tell the same story: that they're overworked, underpaid, passed over for promotions, not appreciated. Racism and sexism are real. We report feeling invisible and discouraged in organizations large and small, and not only in bastions of White-male power. Even within my own corporation, a workplace Mecca for Black women, sisters have had drama.

The guiding principle for keeping your balance in the midst of workplace craziness is a simple one: Have a mission of value, a mission that serves others—one that adds love and light to life—and put that life goal first. Whatever your aspiration is, ask yourself, Is this something I love doing? Will it benefit others? When you can answer yes to these two questions, you'll have found your mission of value, and the benevolent universe will clear away every obstacle in your path.

But you must do your part. You've got to get up each day with every cell in your body thanking God for your life and your mission. You've got to keep your eye on the ball. Being distracted by office politics and pettiness is like stepping up to bat and looking out at the stands. Every pitch, every opportunity, just whizzes by.

The workplace can be an especially wounding place. So you've got to enter it with your guard up, but with your heart open. The challenge is to be in it but not of it while you focus on fulfilling your mission.

Equally challenging is trying to remember that dysfunctional folks bring their pain and dysfunction with them wherever they go. Aware of this fact, you separate the act from the actor, and no one takes you off your path—no crazy co-worker or mean-spirited boss.

Fill your mind with positive thoughts about yourself and your goals, and make realistic plans to take you from here to there. Know why you're working where you are: to gain a skill, to earn money to invest in yourself, to educate your children, to buy a home, to lay the foundation for your own venture—or simply because you love the work. Every thought and move related to your career should be focused in the direction of your dreams. No one's hurtful behavior will fester inside you if you keep your eyes on the prize.

When we're on a mission of value, God gives us a special blessing. Like our ancestors, who always knew The Way even when they couldn't see the light, we are divinely guided. We're surrounded at the highest spiritual level with an aura of protection that disarms any enemy and attracts all we need to succeed. You feel secure, not like an outsider, when you're mission-driven—in solidarity with spirit. You see ingenious ways to turn the wildcats at work into pussycats. No career challenge is greater than you are. Not even a concrete ceiling will keep you from rising.

Passionate and focused, centered in faith and love, serene inside and protected: This is you, a sister on the move, a sister on a mission who can easily brush aside any obstacle to fulfilling the goals you dedicate your life to.

*Quiet time, taking downtime each day should become our lifesaving practice. We are worthy of our own time and deserve to keep for ourselves a share of the energy we devote to others.*

# moments in the light

The visionary educator and founder of what is now known as the Black Women's Health Imperative, Byllye Avery was honored several years ago at the historical Black institution Bennett College for Women. Before an audience of students, educators and women in business and the arts, she challenged us to set aside an hour a day for ourselves. The suggestion caused a collective sigh of relief among us. But who has an unscheduled hour free from having to return calls, check e-mail, do homework, catch up on reading or chores?

Byllye Avery cautioned that we take a big risk in not creating a sliver of space in which to refresh ourselves. She listed the all-too-familiar illnesses, aggravated by self-neglect, our women fall prey to—depression, obesity, hypertension, diabetes, stroke, cancer, heart disease.

The advice brought to mind a magical moment I experienced one summer evening after leaving the office. I was sitting in my living room ready to begin part two of my workday, with newspapers, correspondence, laptop, pens, notebook and phone in position around me, when the setting sun stole my attention. The light was surprising, exquisite and soothing. It had turned the room and the world outside my windows all golden. My dizzying world fell silent. And though I wasn't meditating or in my ritual bath, I felt perfect peace, above the fray, removed from everything else calling for my attention. I'd lived in that apartment for twenty-five years, but not once had I just sat, appreciating the quiet light and miraculous silence that's possible in every God-given day. I let go of the work and lingered in the light.

Our soul and psyche need breathing space—a respite from leaping from one to-do to the next. All of us gathered in the chapel at Bennett knew that Byllye Avery's cautionary charge was on target. We all knew high-achieving women who seemed to have enviable lives—lucrative careers, loving families, homes, money, prestige—but who burned out or broke down and were now working their way back to wellness. Let's not wait to get sick to take a break. Byllye Avery's prescription is preventive. Stress is cumulative, and when we don't stop to rest and restore ourselves, God will lay our body down.

Any quieting activity is restorative. Prayer, meditation, walking, journaling, spiritual reading help us see clearly and hold depression and disease at bay. Moments free of work, worry, stress and strain let our insight rise like sunlight. Quiet time lets us see our way clearly—see what is right, true and next for us, what's critical, what's trivial.

Let's strive for one uncommitted hour daily—sixty minutes when we're not accountable to anyone else. Even the tiniest bit of downtime is delicious and will expand as it is claimed. I want more than stolen moments in the light.

Quiet time, taking downtime each day, should become our lifesaving practice. We are worthy of our own time and deserve to keep for ourselves a share of the energy we devote to others.

*As we mature, we see that the grand prize is in each moment,*
*that life's glory is in the now. Had I been wiser when Babs was alive,*
*my time with my mother would have been so much sweeter.*

# fully here

I have missed much of life's sweetness rushing, half listening to people, wishing they'd get to the point so I could have my say and move on. I rushed my daughter, Shana, to wake, to eat, to sleep. I rushed through visits with my mother because she nagged and wanted to change my ways to hers. But now that Babs is gone, I see that nagging was the only way she knew to love me, to correct and protect me.

As we mature, we begin to see that the grand prize is in each moment, that life's glory is in the now. And who knows how many moments we have left? Had I been wiser when Babs was alive, my time with her would have been so much sweeter.

Where are we going in such a hurry? And what will the physical and emotional outcome be if we're always rushing toward what's next? Living in the future trains us not to be where we are now. With our body in one place and our mind worrying down the road, we are fragmented, estranged from our self. We waste our time on activities that have absolutely no benefit. We misspeak, misplace things, may eat and drink too much, spend too much. Inner listening keeps us present and in touch with our own wisdom, the purest and truest thing we have.

Our goals and efforts shift toward personal and spiritual growth when we begin each day listening to our inner voice. When Spirit speaks, our mind listens. Simply being with my breath while listening inwardly in silence has

ALL ABOUT LOVE

37

changed my life. Practice this simple little ritual regularly, and you'll see what God wants for you and how best to give yourself to that grand vision. Stress and strain disappear, and our activities become effortless and joyful. The most important lesson I have learned is that we must give ourselves to ourselves before giving ourselves away.

Like you, I want to live each moment calm, present and purposeful, not impatient and driven. In communion with others, I want to be fully here. And so I'm learning to listen more, without judging or needing to be right. I want to give heart service, not lip service. I'm trying to slow my conversations, allow more moments for sensing and silence. Supportive silence encourages others to think deeply and speak freely. True communication requires listening with our heart as well as with our ears.

Listening deeply focuses our attention on the present, creating harmony within us, which draws others near. Listening with our heart is the first rule of love. It establishes serenity and joyful relationships. It is the way to inner peace and world peace. As we listen deeply, we gain insight and understanding of ourselves and others. Without a listening heart, there is no respect, no bonding, no intimacy, and no happiness in our relationships.

One of the greatest gifts we can give to ourselves and to one another is undivided attention, the gift of being fully here.

*Your life becomes richer and healthier when you aren't always rushing breathlessly off to some other place. You see that wherever you are, you are in the heart of God—right where you are supposed to be.*

# present time

Throughout most of my life I've harbored a gnawing feeling of discontent, a feeling that whatever point I was at wasn't quite good enough, that there was this nameless something I needed to find to feel complete and content. While it's true that chronic dissatisfaction kept me focused on the future—planning and orchestrating it kept me from settling into a rut—my attention was always divided, my energy fragmented. I missed so many wonderful moments worthy of my concentration, especially as a young mother, because I wasn't fully there. This was true for me even as a schoolgirl.

In class I was always thinking about the end of the day or the end of the term. When I was attending high school, my dreams were about graduation day and being out on my own. Once I got my own apartment, I never really settled in or decorated much because I was in a rush to get married. Then when I got married and saw that it wasn't going to work out, I was soon up and out and on the move again.

The joys of my pregnancy were too quickly replaced by my eagerness to deliver and have my baby home with me. But once Shana Nequai arrived, I became so eager for her to move on to the next stages—to walk, talk, feed herself and become independent—that I missed savoring some of the most precious moments of her development.

I was whizzing through the days on roller skates and not enjoying the ride. So intent on arriving at my next destination, I missed the many pleasures that were right where I was.

Thank God we live and learn. A revelation we all should come to is this: Be where you are. Pay attention to this holy moment;  participate fully. You'll never have an opportunity to live it again. We should thrill to life like children do. I love watching my granddaughter, Amina, and her little friends setting the table, drying dishes or making up their beds. None of these is ever a chore; they get fully engaged, just as they do when they're playing the same game for the fortieth time.

Pause for a moment. Look at the sky, a tree, a building across the street, a plant on your windowsill or a photograph of a loved one. Really look. See and appreciate it as you never have before. Each instant is new, and there is wonderment in everything we do and everything around us. We are just moving too fast to see it or appreciate it. Our distorted view keeps us from celebrating life, which can only be lived one breath at a time.

You and God are one, so serenity resides within you. The wholeness we are searching for lies within us and within the present moment. We lose sight of this mighty connection and the dignity and spirit of all life when our bodies are in one place and our minds are far down the road. The place of peace and assurance we are chasing is right here, in present time, in this instant, now. Be where you are, be aware of yourself and of what a blessing it is to see and sense and feel and touch. Increasingly you will understand the mysteries of life and how to use the many tools at hand for your personal transformation. We have to be still and at peace to hear God's whisperings.

Yes, strive to fulfill your dreams, achieve your goals. But don't miss the significance of this precious and powerful moment on your journey. Acceptance—it's the only place from which you can create satisfaction and joy.

I was racing through my days not because I felt confident and hopeful, but because I was anxious and running from myself. I was looking back with regret and forging ahead in fear, thinking that if I didn't hurry up, life would pass me by. Viewing myself through a prism of false beliefs, I felt vulnerable and convinced myself that because I was without academic credentials, I had to move faster than everyone else to keep my job and to simply keep up. It would be years before I began to fully appreciate how I was growing spiritually and financially, how I was able to assist my family, and all that I was contributing to the magazine, even without a college degree and while raising a child solo.

Often my life has had to spiral out of control for me to slow the speed, listen to the Goddess and let new learning take root in me. Heart palpitations, digestion problems, dry throat—these are the symptoms I'd run with to my dear doctor, Cordia Beverley. She would look at my chart, only to see that I'd had the very same symptoms before and that they were always brought on by the very same things—running and racing and not living in present time.

This I now know: We cultivate clarity when we slow the place. We create a rapport between our body, mind and soul and heal inwardly and outwardly when we make a place for ourselves in our life—for the things that nourish us, like communing with nature and the people we adore.

We were sent here to grow, which requires turning inward for intuition and to tap into resources and strengths lying dormant in us. When we forsake our authentic self for the conflicting messages in the outer world, frustration and anxiety set in.

Before you tune in to the world each day, tune in to you. With your inner world your central focus, you live and breathe easily in present time. Your emotions calm and you won't be reckless, creating circumstances that make your life difficult. Instead your life flows smoothly and you feel at peace. You really listen to what people are saying, and you speak from your heart as your armor falls away.

When we're living in the moment, we don't rush through conversations with our children and our elders. We easily set aside the newspaper or end meaningless telephone talk to give our beloveds all of us. Oh, how I wish I knew this when Shana was a child and my mother was still here.

Ask God for guidance and help to live one day at a time. Your life becomes richer and healthier when you aren't always rushing off breathlessly to some other place. When you're living in the present you are receptive to the wise spirit within you. You are aware that wherever you are, you are in the heart of God—right where you are supposed to be.

# notes

# notes

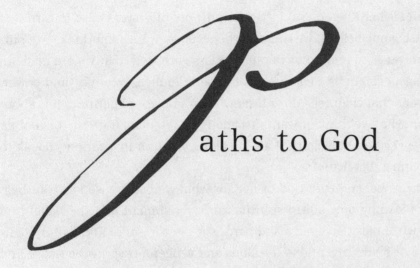

# Paths to God

*Your prayers are for you. God doesn't need your prayers or praise. Prayers are not an insistence: "Listen to me, Holy Spirit, I am speaking," but an invocation: "Speak to me, Holy Spirit, I'm listening."*

# how to pray

Dr. Martin Luther King, Jr., said that the purpose of prayer is not to turn God into some cosmic bellhop we ring for whenever we want something. The purpose of prayer is to remind us of our oneness with God, that we are made in God's image, each of us a channel for divine influence, creativity and power. Prayer opens that channel. Prayer is more than praise and petition. It is about more than what we think or want. It's about selflessness, not self. It is not an insistence: "Listen, Holy Spirit, I am speaking," but an invocation: "Speak to me, Holy Spirit, I'm listening."

Often we bargain with God or beg for what we believe we lack. But begging and pleading only affirm spiritual impoverishment and the belief in a God that withholds "His" grace and parcels it out for praise and flattery. This is the God of man's invention—a jealous and vengeful God, in the image and likeness of what many human beings have become. And this image of a bookkeeping, blessing-rationing, punishing God has been used to instill fear and limit our vision, even to justify Black enslavement, demean women and disempower our people.

But the changeless spiritual truth is this: God is absolute goodness. God is love, and love sustains and supplies everything it has created—the birds of the air, the lilies of the field, the light of the stars and us. Because that's what love does, we don't have to earn it. That's what love is—giving and giving, unceasingly, unconditionally, without waiting for or wanting or needing thanks.

You are safe, even in the eye of the storm. God will never forsake you or take a break from blessing and loving you. Your prayers are for remembering that, for affirming it. Your prayers are for you. God doesn't need your prayers or praise. Nothing you can say or pray will make God love you more. As God's beloved, you have the divine right to live in all the many rooms of the mansion, the right to everything to fulfill your needs and obligations. Your prayers aren't for asking, but for affirming your faith—faith that you, as God's beloved, can be a willing channel for the highest good and that all your needs are met in the right way, at the right time. Praising and thanking don't open God's heart wider. They open yours and fill it with love and gratitude, liberating you from fear, making you wiser, stronger.

Beseeching God for blessings is like searching frantically for your glasses when they're sitting on your face. Our eyes are not the problem; it's our inner vision that's clouded. All life asks of us is this: that we use our gifts wisely and extend our blessings to others.

Don't pray for miracles. Pray for the clarity to see your life as a most miraculous thing. Pray for the desire to love and to give more. These are the secret talismans that multiply our blessings. Make loving and giving your practice, and make that practice your prayer.

*The power of the Presence within enables you to be strong in every circumstance. You will see that God even has under control anyone who would try to harm you.*

# God's got your back

In my life I've exceeded people's early expectations of me. I wasn't an academic star like my brother, Larry, or considered a good girl at home, like my sister, Lil. Our mother found me difficult, and her harshness toward me hurt my heart. When I was 12, "She's not a bad girl . . . ," sweetly crooned by Smokey Robinson, became my anthem and what I wanted my family to know about me.

Who doesn't have a story of childhood pain? The anguish of rejection or loss, the torment of physical and sexual abuse don't pack up and leave easily. If we don't do the work of purging them, their effects will encourage anxiety and phobias to take root in us.

These powerful emotions make us pull back from living fully. We may procrastinate, be crippled by shyness or never take risks to build on our dreams. But trauma from our past doesn't have to drive our future, and we don't have to be free of all our aching memories, all our fears and inner conflicts, to be at peace and move forward. Gaining insight into what holds us back is the first step.

Once I unlocked my deep emotions about my mother's treatment of me, I realized I had taken her harsh judgments much too personally, as children will do. Babs's issues had nothing to do with me. And as my daughter, Shana, knows, parents aren't always wise or right. As I examined Mommy's life over the years, I could see the many layers of pain surrounding her heart, and that she hadn't come to terms with them. I also learned that people limited by their pain can only love others in a limited way. My mother gave me the best she could.

But like pebbles in a bag, we all polish one another. Not feeling the love I hungered for as a youngster has made me compassionate toward others. It also threw me onto my own resources, forced me to grow up quickly and, much to my family's surprise, take responsibility for myself.

We're all acutely aware of the devastating effect families, teachers and administrators can have on the development of children. I have my insecurities and anxieties, and at times they speak loudly, but I won't let them rule me. I can see how they do their work, and that they even have a right to be. They encourage me to seek a deeper relationship with God, to let God guide me and light the way.

Our challenges show us the fences we must climb, the doors we must push open. Insecurity drove me to college for the first time nearly two decades after high school, when I was already editor-in-chief of *Essence*. It was rational insecurity that drove me in the direction I needed to take, praise God. Irrational insecurity is believing that we are insufficient or lacking in any way. Life serves up our lessons in ways we will see and heed.

Name your worst fears: losing your income or home, your health, your lover or your looks. In an instant, any of these can happen and, over time, some surely will. A couple have already happened to me, and I'm still standing strong, enjoying my life more than ever before as it deepens in purpose and meaning.

In the course of a lifetime, everything will fall away from us, but nothing is truly lost. Look deeply, and you'll see how everything is working for the greatest good, that God's got your back and is always moving you toward new possibilities—deeper connections, more meaningful work, greater vitality and excitement, always something new and better. They just may show up in packages that are different from the ones you expected. No matter what life sends your way, just keep stepping toward goodness, toward God.

Trusting God, even in the midst of our upheavals, we grow more powerful, positive and wise. As everything works out in divine order, our faith is strengthened. When we dedicate ourselves to the power responsible for our presence, we become emboldened, more sincere, more strategic and trusting risk takers. We see that God has even our enemies under control.

Living for God connects you to the best of who you are, so you come to your life each day with unshakable faith and a gentle spirit, feeling vibrant, healthy and joyful. You are able to enjoy this exquisite journey and serve your higher purpose, knowing that God's got your back.

*Everything important takes center stage during menopause,
the wisdom years. Hot flashes, a loss of confidence, or
forgetfulness makes us women remember ourselves.*

# what have I forgotten?

Whether it's a headache or heartache, pain is information. It's one way life speaks to us and coaxes us to look more deeply into ourselves to discover what we're doing that's harmful, or what we're not doing to fulfill God's master plan for us. Often pain is the only messenger we heed. It may take an upheaval for us to learn the lessons we didn't learn when they were offered in less dramatic ways.

A purposeful teacher, pain forces us to focus on what we must pay attention to—our bad habits, insecurities, unhealthy relationships, life lived without purpose. Pay no attention to what's disturbing your peace, and suffering becomes your home.

What have I forgotten? That's the decisive question we should ask when physical or emotional distress threatens us.

Not long ago I lost my way, as stress and a crisis of confidence began to overtake me. I'd leave home looking good, polished on the outside, but dying on the inside. It took some time to see that my creeping insecurity, faulty memory and mounting case of the blues were related to menopause and the bushel of responsibilities I was juggling. I would learn that menopause is a powerful and important time in a woman's life, a time of transition, our wisdom years.

Hot flashes and forgetfulness make us remember ourselves. Everything important in our lives takes center stage during menopause; our issues are impossible to ignore. Navigating this untraveled territory, which no woman can avoid, demands that we give birth to new ways of seeing and being. Otherwise, as writer Christina Feldman says, "We sink into an endless destructive grieving." God's instructions to us are everywhere. The language of the Holy Spirit is clear and specific. We only have to tune our ears, open our hearts, trust and love ourselves as much as God loves us.

Whatever shows up in our life is a gift. It's all good. Ultimately, it's all God. Going through menopause helped me to trust and see that there is wisdom hidden in pain. Finally, before my life spun totally out of control, I took the time to slow the pace and ask myself, *What have I forgotten?* The answers are always near. No circumstance can block our way when we reach out to our true source for direction and support. It's in no way complicated. When I asked God for help, my soul awakened and clarity and confidence came.

I had forgotten what I know, what I write and speak about—that to have stability, wisdom and deep inner joy, we must make quiet talks with the Master and exercise a regular part of our lives. When we are busiest, the first things to go are what we need most: meditative or prayer time and aerobic activity, which help keep stress and apprehension at bay. I forgot that I'm more important than what I produce and that my daily challenge is to balance the work ethic and the pleasure principle without guilt. I forgot that the Holy Spirit is glorified when we live in faith and not anxiety—when, no matter what we are going through, we rest secure that God will see us through.

Without daily communion, the hormonal shifts of menopause coupled with the rush of an overscheduled life were overtaking me. I forgot that no matter how many responsibilities and pressured deadlines I have, my first responsibility is to the Giver of Life—to preserve and honor the gift.

How easily we forget to be gentle with ourselves and that each transition we make is a necessary step toward who we will be, a needed move toward new faith, new ideas and new thoughts about what we want next in our life.

We forget that God is with us and hasn't failed us yet. When our strength is low, God's strength is perfect and available to comfort and guide us, to heal our hurts and supply our every need. We forget that ordering our lives doesn't rest on our shoulders alone.

The One is always within us, even when we are unaware of the Presence. This is the purpose of quiet time: remembering to surrender our all to the spirit within. Remembering to turn to God. Remembering to trust God. Remembering to breathe easily so we will find grace and understanding through inner listening. This is what I had forgotten.

*God will never fail you. Keep moving forward*
*in faith. Never give up. Guides seen and unseen,*
*human and divine, will surely open the way.*

# faith in the future

We are the most privileged Black people on the planet. We've been millions of years in the making, hundreds of years being uniquely shaped as we toiled in the forge of this nation. Our free labor helped make this country the wealthiest in the world. Now we nation shapers and wealth makers are in the midst of a time more ripe with opportunities than anyone could have foretold.

It's all within our grasp: Everything our forebears struggled mightily to seize hold of—personal and political power, financial freedom, wholesome relationships, health and happiness—we can have now. We're blessed to have been born when the most turbulent and torturous times for our people are behind us, when the hardest part of our struggle has been waged and won. Surely these are the glory years.

There is a spiritual and mystical revolution under way in the world, making this a most important time on the planet. The potential for love and healing, for creating a better world, has never been greater: The radiant activity of God is pressing to express itself more fully in the world through you. All your greatest desires, the longings hidden deep within your heart, whatever you want to be and experience for the highest good—all these things are trying to come to fruition. A new world is on the way. Get ready. Be willing. God wants to give birth to it through you.

You are a perfect child of God, born for this hour. You have the wisdom, strength and discipline to create the life you want and help move our people forward.

We have the power to change anything—attitudes, habits, illnesses—and to create healthy new models for healing relationships, building wealth, educating our young. We can feed the hungry, house the homeless and eliminate poverty in this land of plenty. The only thing that will impede us is accepting false evidence as real (FEAR). Fear is a powerful force that kills passion and confidence and creates more and more of itself.

For African Americans this can be the second Reconstruction. Advanced technologies have given birth to a new age, throwing open doors of opportunity, making the world our neighborhood. This is the great by-and-by our ancestors prayed for. Look to the legacy and remember who you are, remember those from whom you came and how they got you here. Remember what your grands withstood in order for you to be—that they lost their names, their language, relatives, religion and history, but not their faith in God or their ability to love. Their sacrifices demand that we hold ourselves accountable.

With every breath, surrender your fear to faith. Help God help you: Get fit and focused. Create your plan of action that supports your core values and how you want to live in the next phase of your life. No matter what, don't slack off on executing and building the framework and attending to the critical details on schedule. And commit yourself to giving something back. Believe, as our ancestors did, what has been proven in our history again and again: God never fails us. Just keep moving forward in faith. Guides seen and unseen, human and divine, will always open the way.

*The generations of women before us were taught
the consequences of selfishness. Let ours be the first
to fully understand the consequences of self-neglect.*

# finding our way home

Nearly all of my adult life I have been a pilgrim, a spiritual traveler. I began this quest seeking comfort, inner peace and relief from the fears and forces that were bringing me down. And I've traveled along many paths: religion, prayer and meditation, ancient philosophies and wisdom traditions, psychotherapy, yoga and energy-balancing rituals. I've turned to astrologers, seers and a host of self-help remedies.

The number and variety of supports I've sought in my quest for understanding and happiness may seem extreme, and some of them even foolish: Decades ago when someone on the job was messing with me, a friend suggested I see "the old woman uptown," who blessed a penny with her holy oils, wrapped it in cellophane with a special prayer, and told me to wear it in my shoe for protection. Did the penny have magic? I believed it did, so I let go of my fear. (And by the way, one happy day the woman who was mean to me, and so many other staffers, quit.)

In retrospect, the host of theologies, therapies, strategies and practices I have investigated—and the time, energy and money invested in my search for wisdom and peace—have served me well. Together they have saved my life. Each has in some way drawn me closer to God, to understanding the sacredness of the journey and of what I am yearning for: to feel strong, confident and totally at peace within myself, no matter what's happening around me.

Some of our traditional religious training, steeped in self-negation and punishment, have been draining. Sisters everywhere, in every age group and part of society, have been vulnerable, given the physical, economic and sexual abuse we withstand, and the marginal concern our faith and political communities have for how these death-dealing forces affect our lives. In fact, religious institutions haven't brought justice or wholeness to any society.

But regardless of where we come from, what language we speak or which faith we practice, the spiritual path has provided Black women a refuge from our heartache and anger. Ours is a knowing so ancient, so deep, that a relationship with God fortifies us in the world.

Sisters have traveled the well-worn path of self-sacrifice to the point of feeling guilty about taking any measure for ourselves—of praise, power, time. We've given up much of what we need in order to make ourselves available to others.

Black women, people of African ancestry everywhere must do the mighty work of restoring ourselves, finding our way home, back to God. This is our only salvation. Setbacks and challenges don't mean our life isn't working. They are the turbo-boost we need to make us think, shore up our faith and change.

For me it has been a nearly forty-year spiritual quest. What I've learned is that all God asks of us is this: that we honor ourselves, trust our intuition and heal what hurts, and that human beings of every class treat one another with empathy and love—a task that has proven most difficult for us to fulfill. As my mother would say so often, love is the charity that begins at home.

The generations of women before were taught the consequences of selfishness. Let ours fully understand the consequences of self-neglect.

*Meditation is a lofty word, but practicing it is so simple.*
*There's nowhere to go and nothing to do but sit, relax and listen*
*in silence as the cloak of stillness and peace falls around you.*

# an audience with God

Before her passing, I was blessed to visit Swamini Turiyasangitananda—known worldwide as Alice Coltrane, master musician, composer and widow of John Coltrane—at her ashram in Agoura, California. Spending time with the powerful healer and teacher, surrounded by rolling hills, talking about her spiritual path and the peace she found in meditation, was the reminder I needed to commit more fervently to taking quiet time each morning.

As Sister Alice put it, "Meditation is the pathway to God."

I know she was right. When I neglect to sit in silence for a time, my life swings out of balance. Imbalance hurts. But the pain of feeling out of sorts is life's way of calling us to practice what we forget: First things first: Make being with God a habit, and the world won't crowd or claim you.

Turning away from the world transforms our life in the world into spiritual work. Meditation is a lofty word, but practicing it is so simple. There's nowhere to go and nothing to do but sit, relax and listen in silence. Only when we are relaxed can we see clearly and be creative. We only have to take the time to listen.

Meditation helps us heal and direct our lives. We are able to offer the renewing energy of God in us as a blessing to our family and community simply by turning inward. Meditation makes us stronger and wiser, gives us insight, increases our faith. Regular meditation removes uncertainty and conflict from our life and anchors us in the peaceful, joyful life within us. It's in this blessed silence that I've been able to bring order and meaning to my life, to forgive others and myself. Why would I ever let go of what feeds my soul and brings me sweet serenity and certainty?

Each time we meditate, the awareness of our union with God increases. The cloak of peace and stillness falls around us, and in time it envelops us completely. We begin to trust that no matter how things may appear in the physical world, at the spiritual level nothing in us is missing or broken.

God adores us, and everything in our life is in divine order. When you awaken each morning, lie still for a few minutes and take time to remember that you are always in the heart of God.

**A Simple Meditation Practice**

Choose a special place to commune with God in the morning, before the day rushes in. Sister Alice recommended sitting or lying in the same place each day, because over time it increases the spiritual energy there. Then just breathe. Your breath is God in you. Let the warmth of it caress and bless every part of your body, from your feet that touch the earth, to your womb that nurtures life, to your eyes that admit the world. Send the warm healing energy of your breath anywhere you have pain or illness. It will help heal and restore you. Send your breath to your heart. Feel your chest filling with love and joy, peace and gratitude. Keep breathing. Keep listening.

In our stressed and hurried lives, an audience with God is too important to miss. Let us recommit ourselves to sitting in silence for a time each day. The Spirit of Peace is within you, awaiting you. Always.

*The purpose of Jesus in his life on earth was to leave us a map of the journey to faith. Now we must follow his footsteps and trust in his words: "It is not I, but the Father within, who does the work."*

# every step you take

A weary traveler, high in the Himalayas, was trying to reach the mountaintop when he met a sage along one of the steep, craggy paths. The frustrated, fearful traveler asked the sage which of the many paths would take him to his destination. The sage pondered, then replied, "Simply make certain that every single step you take is in the direction of the summit, and you will get there."

At times we all feel like weary travelers unsure of which way to turn. The road to the summit isn't straight and smooth. It twists and changes course, with unpredictable events around each bend. But we have courageous travelers whose steady steps have already marked the way. Treading the path through the blood of the slaughtered while subjected to odious acts of violence, they held fast to their faith in God, a vision of freedom, and trust in our future. Like Malcolm and Martin, Marcus Garvey, Mary McLeod Bethune, Harriet Tubman, the woman called Moses, we must take care, no matter how winding the road, to place our feet in the direction of our intentions.

Not every wanderer is lost. Jesus wandered the desert for years, seeking the wisdom of the sages. He applied what he learned and passed quickly into Christhood. Yet we make an idol of Jesus, rather than placing our own feet in the imprint of his steps. The purpose of Jesus in his life on Earth was to leave us a map of the journey to faith. Now we must follow his footsteps and trust in his words: "It is not I, but the Father within, who does the work."

If we have unwavering faith while moving steadily toward our intentions, all that threatens us along the way will go into hiding or be revealed as the impostors they are. That's because faith insists that we stop casting ourselves in the role of victim. It reminds us who we are and what we came here to do. It shores us up so that we stop giving our power away.

Alienated from this inner power and trust, I've sometimes wandered off course, unsure of my place, feeling stressed, depressed and weary. Then I remember this: Everything in our life can be a pathway to God. We have to trust life, trust each moment, trust ourselves. I know now that each wandering experience was a necessary one. I needed to examine my life more deeply until the inner roadblocks—my fears, my hurtful habits, the strain of not following my heart—were illuminated. The way to clarity and healing is to ask ourselves at each step, Is my energy aligned with my intention? Am I placing my feet rightly along the road?

We have a mighty work before us. We have to open wide the pathway to healing and opportunity for the millions of our children suffering on our watch. Like Jesus and our ancestors, we must stay focused and have walk-on-water faith, which is not the same as passive acceptance. Having faith means working your plan with a steadfast trust in God's love and protection, knowing that all you'll ever need has been placed within your reach. You have only to keep your eyes on the summit and your feet rightly placed. God is guiding your way. Trust that, and keep on stepping.

*No matter how far from home we have wandered or how distant the goal, with a steady pace and perseverance we will arrive. All God's children have traveling shoes. Venture forth; the bridge will be there.*

# the bridge will be there

My heart-attack scare—when I was 24, a new mother and newly separated—will be forever etched in my memory as the bridge to a new way of thinking and living. I was broke, afraid, having chest pains and such difficulty breathing that I headed straight to the emergency room that Sunday morning. The young physician who examined me discovered that my heart was fine. My diagnosis was anxiety, not heart failure. To save the carfare, I started the long walk home from Manhattan to The Bronx, grateful but still shaken.

Along the way, I stopped at a church and found a place in the back of the sanctuary, where I heard a revolutionary sermon about the futility of looking outside ourselves for salvation. "God is alive in you," The Reverend Alfred Miller kept reminding the congregation. As I walked home, my mind swirled with questions about what the minister had said. *God is alive in me?* I questioned, pondering the idea and wondering what it could mean in my life. What if, just like the Macombs Dam Bridge beneath my feet, holding me above the swirling currents of the Harlem River, there was a divine bridge within me that I could use to cross over the emotional distress, fear and anxiety that were threatening to pull me under?

Often I think about that day and about how everything in our life is always in divine order. All roads lead home. Even when we feel lost, even when we're going in circles, bumping into walls, we're finding our way home. God never stops guiding and protecting us or twisting and turning us, pushing and pulling us, sending whatever it takes to awaken our faith and our will to shape our own lives.

That Sunday I saw the path opening before me, and how the creative power of our thoughts, words and actions gives form to the energy within and around us. Whatever we radiate, we attract. What we express, we create a channel for receiving: "Thou shalt decree a thing and it shall be established unto thee." It's a spiritual law, as immutable as the law of action and reaction in physics.

My heart scare was a head trip. My negative outlook was making me sick. "I can't" had become my mantra. But we can. Life is an adventure with mountains, valleys and roadblocks. And we never know how fit we are to navigate them all until we have to.

Since that Sunday I have used walking as physical exercise and meditation. It brings balance to my crazy-busy life, helps me stay fit and savor the company of my own soul. My walking ritual strengthens my faith in the bridge within and beneath us and helps me see how placing one foot before the other gets us there.

No matter how far from home we are or how distant the goal, with a steady pace, patience and perseverance we will arrive. All God's children have traveling shoes. Venture forth; the bridge will be there.

*Send a loving thought across the room to a sourpuss, and God will bless you. Pledge never again to scream at your children, but to call them precious, beautiful, responsible and smart, and that's how they will show up.*

# love like you mean it

I've watched the spirit of love work its magic in the life of one of the most loving souls I know, my friend Judy Owens. Judy and her soul mate, Grady, had a thirty-year marriage made in heaven. They ran the famous Black-owned resort King's Lodge, which became the Betty Shabazz Wholistic Retreat Center.

The property, in upstate New York, had been in the Owens family for 65 years. Then occupancy dwindled, Grady died, and the lodge went into foreclosure. Judy's life seemed to unravel. But even when we are unaware of it, we are in God's care. It was everyone's joy to watch the miracle unfold: At the eleventh hour the lodge was sold, and Judy went from an uncertain future to financial independence. And once again she's receiving the love she has always given. I remember her asking, "How could this happen to me twice?" Judy had met the second love of her life—at age 63! And when I asked the handsome Dr. Lindley Smith, now Judy's husband, what it was about her that swept him off his feet, he simply said, "Her light. I saw it from across the room." And he couldn't resist it.

Judy is a gentle spirit, so warm and openhearted. She's committed to service, and is one of the kindest people I've ever met. She loves like she means it. And so she is loved; life continues to bless her.

Love is healing, irresistible, the magnet for blessings. Love is our spiritual DNA, the blueprint encoded in the human spirit that creates and sustains us. Loving-kindness is the only path to happiness. We're happiest when we're most loving—happier even than when others are loving toward us. Keep your mind focused on love, and let your actions stem from love and you will have a deep sense of contentment.

Loving is spiritual practice and how we stay conscious of our connection to God. When all is well in our inner world, everything in our outer world flows easily. Treat yourself kindly; love yourself fully. This is the wellspring of every good thing that comes to you and through you to others.

The great paradox is that our cup is filled by our outpouring of love. Giving wisely only increases our supply. Our children don't need $250 sneakers or another video game. Family and friends don't need us to work till we're worn thin. The great gifts everyone needs from us are free and healing: our wisdom and understanding, our kindness and forgiveness, our encouragement, our smile.

Send a loving thought across the room to that sourpuss boss, and God will bless you. Pledge never again to scream at your children, but to call them precious, beautiful, responsible and smart, and that's how they will show up in the world, modeling you.

Love like you mean it—actively, joyfully—and soon your heart will overflow with happiness. Your every step will be divinely guided. And you'll see that the universe will open up, as it has for Judy, and pour forth blessings greater than anything you ever imagined.

*The everyday work of living is sacred. Our lives grow peaceful and each moment becomes more meaningful when we see all that we do—washing the dishes, paying bills, helping others—as an offering to God.*

# the everyday sacred

I led our advance team to Brazil, where *Essence* was planning a magical voyage of self-discovery for our readers. There, where the rhythm of samba rises up like a race memory, and the spirit of the Motherland lives in the rituals and exotic aromas of Afro-Brazilian cooking, we reveled in the sensuous, the cultural and the mysterious. We learned a great deal from sisters and brothers who have held on to our root culture over the centuries and celebrated it.

Who doesn't fall in love with Brazil, this lush country and its warm, friendly people? What a joy it was to return to Brazil a few months later with nearly 200 *Essence* readers and some of our most revered healers and teachers, who helped us map the journey to wholeness in the midst of a culture where spirituality is an integral part of everyday life.

In Bahia's Pelourinho District—where our ancestors laid the ocher cobblestone streets and in the eighteenth century built The Church of the Black People—I marveled at how folks in every kind of dress moved easily through the Catholic church, laughing, chatting, stopping to buy food from the woman with a big pot of something good cooking just inside the sanctuary doors.

And at Cachoeira we visited members of the Sisterhood of Boa Morte, the renowned Afro-Brazilian religious order and the oldest society of Black women in the Americas. Formed in 1820 by freed slaves, the Sisterhood was dedicated to buying freedom for elderly Black women so they wouldn't die in servitude. After we discussed the program the Sisterhood would host for us, one of our guides asked the leader of the distinguished women to dance the traditional samba.

What a memorable moment it was. We formed a circle in the vestibule of the church around the 93-year-young high priestess, clapping in rhythm as she moved joyfully, sensually, with power and grace, her feet speaking an ancient language of movement. We all caught the spiritual sweetness radiating through her and joined in. In that world the practice of spirituality is radically different from the one we know, and certainly from the one I came of age in attending Catholic school, where the lines between the hallowed and the unconsecrated were clearly drawn.

That afternoon in Bahia as we danced in the vestibule, I was reminded that all of life is sacred: not just the time we spend practicing the religious rituals we've been taught to use to honor God, but also the time spent preparing a meal, washing dishes and clothes, paying our bills, helping the kids with their homework. The everyday work of living is sacred. Our lives grow peaceful and each moment becomes more meaningful when we see all we do as an offering to God.

Our life is a gift from God. When we are mindful of this truth, greater love and acceptance emerge from within us. We understand that each moment merits our attention, awe and gratitude. The world around us relaxes. We stop fussing and fearing, judging others and second-guessing ourselves so much.

Contentment and joy don't come from having all the treats we crave in the candy store; they spring spontaneously from being at peace with what *is* in our lives—whatever we're doing, wherever we are, whomever we're with.

Mindfulness helps us make the mental and emotional shifts. As God's highest creation, we have dominion and also the responsibility to choose wisely how we will show up in the world each moment. We can get evil when our partner irritates us or when the baby cries at 3:00 A.M., or we can practice understanding and compassion and give thanks for having a love beside us, and a new life to cherish.

As we hold in our hearts and mind that all of life is sacred, we begin to approach each situation with care and curiosity. We grow stronger and softer at once. We're not at war with life. We are instead in the flow of life, at peace with the everyday. In Brazil I was reminded of the sanctity of life and of our responsibility to oppose anything that taints it—poverty, violence and all injustice.

We are living in a world of opportunity and choice. Let's stand for what is sustainable—life lived with love and respect for all. Let's stand for the sacred—gently but firmly.

# notes

# notes

# elf-love and Social Action

*Every crisis is temporary. No matter what the challenge, God is the answer. No matter what the need, God is the fulfillment. I promise myself to remember.*

# I promise myself

When I joined *Essence*, I was 24, parenting solo and struggling on every front. Anxious, sad and lonely, I was desperately trying to keep it all together for my precious little Shana, while answering the charge to work hard and help build the fledgling magazine. I didn't understand then that every crisis is a call from God—a summons to deep reflection, life-changing decision making and commitment to spiritual practice.

I know this now. One of the joys in growing older is gaining the wisdom and confidence to heed the call of your soul—before life slaps you upside the head again and again. I've promised myself to be accountable and responsible for who I am and what I want to become. My psyche and soul have suffered so from "hurry sickness." Some friendships, too. But life is good; in each moment we get to choose again.

So after twenty-five years of writing In the Spirit, I knew I needed to pause, to stop writing for a moment to catch my breath, read, reflect and listen. I wanted to spend time with some of our master healers and teachers exploring how Black people can learn to cherish ourselves more, have healthier intimate relationships, and knit to our own vision and purpose the well-being of our community. I also wanted to share their wisdom with you.

Refreshed and challenged by these conversations with some of our finest minds, I returned to writing In the Spirit knowing deeply that this is a time of transformation for you and me. It's our time to rise, Black women's time to reawaken a sureness of purpose within ourselves and within our people. Vigilance, optimism and our pointed participation are so needed now.

Whisper these few promises to your soul in the quiet of each morning, or create your own affirmations. This will make a sacred space for healing and inner cheering. It will help you find and follow the divine right path life has prepared for you:

• I promise myself to live by the authority of my own soul today and to practice being my own best friend and motivator.

• I promise to speak to myself kindly and to give myself the attention and nourishment I need.

• I promise to remember that others' opinions, judgments and deeds can't diminish me. I promise not to hide out or play it safe, but to bring my open heart and Master mind to each moment with confidence.

• I promise to believe in myself and in the genius of my people.

• I promise myself to live this day with joy and enthusiasm, to allow only love and light to flow through me no matter who or what life sends my way. Everywhere I look I will see beauty and possibility, and I let my light shine in service to my people, giving joyfully from a full cup.

• I promise myself to remember that every circumstance is a pathway to God, and that every crisis is temporary, lasting not a moment longer than it takes for me to surrender it to God and ask for a divine solution.

• I promise myself to remain faithfully aware that God is always here, with and within me. That no matter what the challenge, God is the answer. No matter what the need, God is the fulfillment. I promise myself to remember.

*Let God be God in you. Practice putting your faith in these empowering words: "Thy will be done" and "Though the earth do change, I shall not be moved."*

# let God

"Let go and let God."

We know these words so well, but putting our faith in them is a challenge for us all. So often, without our being aware of it, our negativity blinds us to the good and the gifts that are always around us. How we experience life is always directed by our thoughts; they are creative energy with the power to embolden or terrify us.

We are more than we seem, much more than mere channels for God's activity. We are the very activity of God on earth, created to be earth angels—the eyes, ears and material body of the Master. Spiritual teacher Paramahansa Yogananda, a leader in introducing Eastern philosophy and yoga to the Western world, called us an "Ocean of Life," each of us a tiny wave. "When in every action you think of Him before you act, while you are performing the action, and after you have finished it," he said, God in you is revealed to you. "You must work, but let God work through you; this is the best part of devotion," the revered Indian Guru added. "If you are constantly thinking that He is walking through your feet, working through your hands, accomplishing through your will, you will know Him."

Every circumstance in our lives is meant to help us end conflict and suffering, awaken us to our powerful spiritual nature and the presence of the Infinite within our bodies and behind everything we encounter. There is no need to doubt or fear, only to connect with the Source.

Not long ago, I was racing to catch a flight to Los Angeles. New York City traffic was at a standstill. As my shoulders began to tense and my stomach tightened, I remembered that there was no need to race. This time, unlike most other times when I travel, my meetings and events weren't scheduled for within hours of my arrival but for the next afternoon.

*Practice what you preach, Suga'*, I told myself. *Everything is in divine order; just let go and let God.* I would do my best to make the flight, but if I missed it, I'd simply catch the next one.

I arrived at bustling JFK International Airport just minutes before the flight was scheduled to depart, found the least busy person at the ticket counter, and quickly asked him to call the gate and request that they hold my seat. "No way ya gonna make that flight, lady," was his indifferent response. "Please try for me," I implored. "Forget about it," he returned.

Not a chance, I thought, as I headed toward the steps I'd have to climb before making the quarter-mile trek to the gate, with correspondence, newspapers, my computer and the clothing I needed for my week's stay in tow. But I was cool.

I moved swiftly and surely, telling myself to breathe deeply and rhythmically and surrender the outcome to Spirit. How confident we feel, how smoothly life unfolds, when we see that we have choices, and that nothing we need is at risk. Though anxiety would have overtaken me had I feared missing the flight, I witnessed how easily things come together—synchronicity, it's called—when we consciously let God handle the details—keep the faith and expect the best.

All along our path God has placed guardian angels to help us: A woman carrying only a handbag helped me up the stairs with my gear; a brother in a motorized cart breezed me through a tunnel and the terminal. When we got stuck at security, he urged me to go on to the gate—he would manage the bags and meet me there. I arrived at the gate as they were about to give my seat away.

Sitting comfortably in that seat as we ascended through a canyon of cotton-white clouds, I marveled at how mysterious and finely choreographed life is and how much our attitude has to do with the way our experiences unfold. Fear is having faith in false evidence—in the illusion of random hazards, chaos and setbacks rather than in the reality of divine order. Fear blinds us to the truth that whenever you take a few positive steps, God gives you wings. How different our lives would be if we'd just remember our interconnectedness with the Holy Spirit, our Oneness.

How's your life working? Is there carnage in the Black community in your town? And what about the killing field the earth has become? Everywhere there is hunger and poverty, government dishonesty, loss of liberties, terrorism, war, theft of the national wealth. The pain in the world is an echo of our own pain, the life-destroying consequences of our forgetfulness and fear. We are learning the hard way that we must integrate the spiritual, our faith in God, into every aspect of our life.

Women and men committed to a spiritual life have to honor the bringing of peace and harmony to our personal, political, sexual and social worlds. We can't say we love God and then cuss someone out. Can't say we are serving God and then not stand strong for justice. Our spiritual practice is irrelevant if we're just uttering, "Have a blessed day," but doing nothing to bring blessings to the people suffering all around us—with the most vulnerable of these the children.

It's downright destructive to our community for Black women to support preachers whose ministries are all about show, building emporiums and taking the spoils of the pulpit without leading their congregations to do God's work. Throughout our history, and until recent years, worship service was about praising God and employing strategies to loosen the racist chokehold on Black progress. Today, we need literacy and job training and mentors for our young. Today's Civil Rights Movement demands that our churches and temples be dedicated to after-school homework help for neighborhood children, turning failing schools into safe, top-tier learning environments, as well as to embracing brothers and sisters coming out of prison and helping them find their footing, stay drug free, get workforce-ready and become entrepreneurs.

Having a true spiritual life requires more than having compassion for ourselves. We must also have compassion for others, must become emboldened with the courage needed to act on behalf of those struggling along the margin of our margin as we deepen our understanding of Oneness. A true spirituality has no boundaries between the inner and outer life. And it is revolutionary when directed toward justice. The only way God can end conflict, domination and suffering on Earth is through us. We are the light in this long disheartening night. Courage comes easily when you have a sense of higher purpose, and the fact is, few things are as fulfilling and empowering as fighting for social change.

Be on guard against fearful thinking every moment of your life. The minute you feel fear, remember to let go of it and let God handle the matter. Every time you succeed in turning away from fear, you strengthen your trust in God and your ability to live by the Authority imbued in you. Practice giving way to the Holy Spirit in the small things that happen to you each day. Challenge yourself to see God everywhere, in everyone and in all that comes your way. This will change your life; it will melt the fear that has held back love and joy.

No matter what the emptiness, God is the fullness. Practice putting your faith in these empowering words: "Thy will be done." Echo the words of the Psalmist, "Though the Earth do change, I shall not be moved." Let God be God as you.

*With our mind we have the ability to create something from nothing. This is what it means to be made in God's image and likeness. This is what gives us dominion.*

# what's the plan?

Where do you see yourself a year from now? Five years from now? Where do you want to be and how would you like to be living and loving? If no clear image comes to mind, don't panic. Get busy!

It's been said a hundred ways: "Without vision, the people perish." "If you fail to plan, you plan to fail." "If you don't know where you're going, any road will take you there." But is *there* where you want to be? Nature always fills a vacuum with something. But the chance that that something will magically and perfectly fulfill your nameless desires is as good as your chance of hitting a lottery jackpot.

Entropy is the natural tendency of things to fall apart. But if we adopt instead a positive vision and couple it with our own creative effort, organization and commitment, we won't slip into chaos.

Whatever you want out of life you must first envision. See it clearly. Name it, proclaim it, then make detailed plans to bring it to fruition. Dreams precede reality. There's no human invention that was not first a vision, an image in the mind, a thought, a concept, a word.

On the edge of the savannah our ancestors donned antelope masks and danced the drama of a successful hunt. People in caves painted images of their desires on the walls. Harriet Tubman had to imagine herself free before mustering the courage to formulate a plan to escape from slavery and return again and again to lead others to freedom.

What we focus on increases in our lives. Our thoughts and words have creative power, giving form to formless energy all around us. When we think or speak negatively about ourselves, our body, our talents and intellect, we create the conditions to bring it to fruition.

There is nothing inadequate or haphazard about you. You are God's offspring, called into being at this time, in this place, because you have lessons to learn and gifts to give. But the living ain't easy. Each day we must make a conscious effort not to see ourselves in a mirror distorted by racism, sexism or our painful life experiences. Those forces would only have us deny ourselves and our power. See the full beauty of who we are: We are more than simply survivors. We are thrivers, powerful and capable women and men born for this hour.

Our forebears were the mothers and fathers of civilization, the initiators of language, of community, of art and science. But sadly, ours are the first generations throughout the Diaspora to relinquish fundamental ancestral values—respect, discipline, responsibility to the community. Consequently, we are the first generations to allow our children to lose ground. It makes sense—life-saving sense—that once again we embrace the morals of a culture that saved us from annihilation.

There is a critical need for us to be clear about the future we want. Can we work together and hold a vision of what we want to achieve, and fashion a plan to make it real? Can we do it in the tradition of those who envisioned a new world and actually set about creating it?

John's Gospel makes it clear: "In the beginning was the Word." It is this ability to create something from nothing—from a vision held in the very silence of our mind—that gives us dominion. That is what it means to be made in God's image and likeness. You have power—God's power in you. All you have to do is use it. What's your plan?

*Our thirst for spiritual growth is encouraging Black women to meet at the well. These sisterhood gatherings are the spaces we claim to drink the life-giving waters.*

# claiming a space

Our foremothers taught us a lot by their example. But over time we've fallen into forgetfulness. We've forgotten our power, our passion and our place. We've forgotten that the feminine is sacred and that God has given us everything we need to do the work we were sent here to do. We sisters should be organizing and raising hell about the things that are hurting us and our children most. We should be working together in joy, love and celebration to create a healing agenda and a new beginning for our people.

The great benefits that millions of us enjoy today don't come from nothing. They have grown out of a long and glorious legacy of mutual love, faith and commitment, which gave our foremothers the courage to stand strong together and petition for justice during times much harder and harsher than these.

Few books documenting African American history include the tremendous contributions of Black women. In her important book *Too Heavy a Load*, Deborah Gray White details how at the turn of the twentieth century, though they faced lynching, mob violence and segregation, Black women organized locally and nationally and stepped forward with a plan to help move the race forward. Organized in 1892 in Washington, D.C., the Colored Women's League called for "a united black womanhood to solve the race's problems." In a short time it had branches in the South and as far west as Kansas City.

In 1905 the 74 members of the exclusive Tuskegee Women's Club weren't too sophisticated to do grassroots work. They visited incarcerated Black men, taking them food and clean clothing, and they lobbied state officials for prisoners' rights. In time, these women started a night school, established a reading room for boys, and taught women how to buy land and build their own homes.

Bodacious sisters in Savannah organized a community watch, deputized themselves, wore badges and patrolled their own neighborhoods. Professor White says there was little that Black women then didn't organize themselves to do, and they did it all without phones or fax machines, computers or the Internet.

Today, our deep thirst for spiritual communion is pushing Black women to meet at the well. We may call it our book club, sister circle, study group or just hanging with our girls, but these sisterhood gatherings are the spaces we claim to speak the truth about our lives and drink the life-giving water. There's even a Los Angeles society named Sisters at the Well, a group of committed Black women, organized by my friend Barbara Perkins and doing powerful spiritual and activist work. However we gather—in small, intimate groups or large councils, in sororities or coalitions—we are called to have on our agenda a project that benefits our people.

Across the nation there are thousands of organizations and religious institutions empowered by Black women, but there isn't one single issue, not one piece of legislation we can say we as a group are organized around in a meaningful way. When women shrink from dealing with life-threatening issues, the community decays and the whole society falls apart.

We women are the keepers and carriers of culture; we're the soul of our households and communities, and they will be no more or no less than what we bring to them. We are the leaders we've been waiting for, as writer and activist June Jordan reminded us throughout her life, cut short by breast cancer. We must stand up, must be proactive in determining the behavior and moral tone that will shape our lives going forward.

Nothing is more important to the future of our children, and the healing and growth of our community, than that we Black women think critically and move swiftly, using all the oars we have in the water to pull smartly in the same direction. We women are being called to reenchant the world.

*It's time for the Goddess to awaken from patriarchy's trance. Time to make the mental shifts needed to own the fullness of our Divine Feminine power.*

# free the goddess within!

No more fear. No more wrestling with lies that make you feel less than God's beloved or the unique and ravishing woman you are. No more betrayals of the Goddess, our Divine Feminine power—Mother Love—the grace God fired the human heart with to balance our all-too-human aggression.

Mother Love, Big Mama, Ma' Dear, Earth Mother—the names of the Goddess are legion. Her power is sacred. Her nature is to bring forth life, to love and preserve it. What affects Mother affects all of creation. When women are oppressed, debased and devalued, the people suffer, life in the village erodes. But when we lift the veil of mental blindness and step into our power, we not only gain the clarity and wisdom that erase doubt and sorrow, but our healing presence also brings new life and nourishment to all around us.

I was reminded of this recently when I stopped by a favorite boutique. As I greeted the lovely young sister who is the manager, I saw at once that something within her had shifted. She wasn't disheartened about her challenges as she had been in the past—juggling work and mothering solo, strategizing how to start her own business. Instead, she was aglow. "I've stepped into my feminine power and the glory of being a Black woman," she declared. "I see it, I feel it, it's mine, I own it! The blind spot I've lived with is gone."

She went on to share that she'd never thought well of herself and had secretly despised her looks—her blue-black skin, full nose, lush body. One day her little girl, who is her mirror image, came home from school crying because classmates had said she was ugly. Suddenly my young friend realized that by accepting society's judgments about her own looks and worth, she had both robbed herself and her daughter. Seeing her eight-year-old struggling with her looks, repeating the old poisonous negations of Black women's beauty kept alive by mainstream culture—and ours as well—was the wake-up call she needed to work at consciously loving and celebrating how God had created her.

As the young mother saw clearly, it's time for the Goddess to awaken from patriarchy's trance. Time to make the mental shifts needed to own the fullness of our Divine Feminine power. Ask the Goddess within to give you wisdom and faith, to show you how every person and situation is sent to add to your understanding and peace. Give the Goddess permission to live in you, to show you how to end your suffering and the suffering of our children, how to bring peace into your home and our community. Only Divine Mother Love will reverse the deadly decline into global madness that ignorance, greed and neglect have caused.

Visionary sisters are stepping forward to lead and help their people heal: Ellen Johnson-Sirleaf in Liberia and Luisa Diogo in Mozambique. Women are also heads of state in many other countries. The world is in desperate need of the hearts and minds of women, and the feminine energy within every human spirit, to reclaim and renew our world.

God adores you. It's as simple as that. Nothing else matters. The Divine Feminine principle, Mother Love, is our hidden wealth, the ultimate power in the universe. Bring love, Mother Love, only that, and everything you're struggling with—embracing your beauty, believing in yourself, loving yourself, forgiving, letting go of emotional and physical challenges, bringing peace to your household—will be made easier.

Free the Goddess! We need her love and light to heal our world.

*This is no time to dream small. Our fears and time pressures must not win. Not when the life of our community hangs in the balance. God wants plenty more from you; this is why you are still here.*

# pieces of a dream

During my mother's precious last nine months, as her health was slipping, I lingered with her shared memories, her parting thoughts. Like most elders, she had grown insightful, wise and reflective—expressing gratitude for her 83 years, for living to see her children grown, for a good life overall. The sadness she did feel, she said, was because she'd abandoned her own dreams. Babs spent her life helping my father build a business, his dream, and meeting the daily demands of caring for her family. Her own dreams she put off forever.

Our dreams cannot be actualized unless we breathe life into them. They require open air. Sunlight. Action. Attending to one piece of a dream at a time is the way we bring it into being.

As a young mother, I started a cosmetics company after making a plan and putting it on a two-year timeline. With my earnings stashed away, I began working the plan step-by-step. I investigated cosmetology schools, selected the most affordable one nearby, and enrolled. When I completed the course, I sold cosmetics at a department store to learn the retail end of the business. Then I struck out on my own. My company was doing well when I interviewed at *Essence* with then editor-in-chief Ida Lewis for the position of freelance beauty editor. But today, like Babs, I struggle to find the time, energy and commitment to follow my dreams: I want to learn and teach how to turn whole communities around, how to revitalize and stabilize them.

We can't let the curtain close on this drama of our delay. Our fears and time pressures must not win. Not now. Not when the life of our community hangs in the balance, when our rights and freedom are eroding, when no job is guaranteed. Not at this critical time when we must bring America to its senses and war to its knees. This is no time to dream small.

God wants plenty more from us, which is why we're still here. Let's create a vision statement that supports our dreams, then map them out and begin organizing each day's priorities around our vision.

The future is ours to choose: Virtually everything we want to achieve rests on our understanding and consciously exercising this power. Whatever we believe sends an order for action to our subconscious and the universal mind that dutifully make it manifest.

We can change the order. Declare: I am a child of God, wise, guided and loved. I choose health, wealth, happiness and sweet companionship. This is what we should see and say each day. Looking back, Mommy realized she could have asked the family for more help in running the household. Finally learning to love and be generous with herself, Babs said, was her greatest lesson, one she wished she'd learned early on.

Today this is also our urgent need: to align self-love and care with our dreams and responsibilities. In the end, we will find that loving ourselves and pursuing our dreams are the same glorious effort.

*You are more than enough. Creation makes no mistakes.*
*What a miracle! More than 6 billion people on the planet,*
*and God created every one of us as a divine original.*

# loving what God made

"Everything in the universe has a purpose," writer Marlo Morgan said. "There are no misfits, there are no freaks, there are no accidents. There are only things we don't understand."

I have pondered these words often—relied on them to shore me up when insecurity has overtaken me, when I've been made to feel fearful and sick, believing that I'm not enough as I am. Spirit makes no mistakes. What a miracle! More than six billion people on the planet, and God created every one of us as a divine original.

Feeling capable and powerful, feeling your wholeness and joy—this is the exquisite freedom kept alive in just one way: understanding that nothing is more significant than being yourself fully and immensely. When you live your life on your own terms, absent silent self-sacrifice and someone else's plan, you free yourself from trying to convince others that you're more than you are. You know that who you are is more than enough. When you release the need to be right, or first, or perfect, you break the chains that lock down your happiness, you untie the knot in your stomach, undo the traumas of the past.

I grew up in a family in which I felt as if I didn't fit. Born to quiet, conservative Caribbean parents, I was curious and chatty, longing for cuddles, kisses and smiling eyes. My openness and exuberance seemed to frighten my steady, sturdy parents, mature people who didn't like to be touched. Hungry for affection, I sought it outside my home, in dangerous places, in the arms of boys in my East Harlem neighborhood.

I'm fortunate to have survived. I wish I'd realized as a child that I wasn't inferior or shameful, that my feelings weren't wrong. My needs were simply different from anything my parents or the nuns at my Catholic school could understand.

Too many of us lose ourselves in families and institutions that push us toward sameness. Who we become isn't who we are, but who we've been taught we should be. Through reward and punishment, through repetition, guilt and fear, we are molded by people, blind to the fact that our world works in Divine Order when we live from our heart. This push toward standardization—in our families, religious communities, in business, government and media—stunts creativity and breeds frustration, alienation and chaos. In our mind, something about us is always wrong and needs fixing.

But freedom, joy and spiritual power come from being fully yourself. Figure out who you are and do you. What's true for you feels good, natural. The right moves come easily. Don't try to become what you're not. Instead, tell yourself you love everything about you—your looks, your preferences and idiosyncrasies. Look in the mirror, into your own eyes. Praise yourself from the inside out, from head to toe. See your body, whole and perfect, no matter its shape or condition. Love what God made.

A new world is on the way, and to give birth to it, we must honor this sacred contract with ourselves. Spirit is calling you to pledge allegiance to yourself, to the gift of life, to your unique personhood. Not to a flag, militarism or materialism, not to religious leaders who demonize those who worship differently, not to crusaders who campaign against people who choose to love differently. God makes no mistakes. Everyone is unique. And there's room for all of us in the kingdom.

*Women do two thirds of the world's work, but earn one tenth of the world's wages and own less than one one-hundreth of its wealth. This injustice holds all of humanity hostage.*

# carrying your own head

This is what I learned early on: Disrespect yourself, and other folks, even your family, will disrespect you, too.

We teach people how to treat us by how we treat ourselves. Without standards and parameters, anyone or anything can show up in your life. I love how the Ghanaian theologian and author Mercy Amba Oduyoye puts it: "My grandmother taught me that I must always carry my own head."

We are all here on purpose, with God-given assignments: We have lessons to learn, work to do, gifts to give. But we can't fulfill our purpose handicapped with attitudes and behaviors that aren't in accord with what God wants for us. To receive the abundance that flows from the Holy Spirit, we have to cooperate with the source of our blessings. Why are we here if not to use our innate gifts and talents, and to live out our purpose? But how can we achieve these if we do not carry our own head?

It's often a struggle to get other people's notions of who we are and how we should be out of our heads. This is particularly true for women. We are taught to distrust what is essential to our happiness and self-esteem—our inborn wisdom and intuition—and to overvalue superficial and ephemeral things, like our looks and other people's opinions.

In every culture, women struggle against violence and inequity. Often the place where we should feel the safest and most respected—our home—is where we're violated most severely. We do two thirds of the world's work, but earn one tenth of the world's wages and own less than one one-hundredth of its wealth. And each week we sisters, hungry for communion, flock to houses of worship built by us, supported by us, where an all-knowing male minister won't allow a woman in "his" pulpit.

When we carry our own head, we have the power to call out sexism and misogyny wherever they exist—even in the untruths imposed upon our powerful sacred texts over the centuries by redactors. The unenlightened interpretation of the Creation story in Genesis, for instance, suggests that Eve's uncontrollable sensuality is responsible for "the fall" and that women are therefore the source of impurity and death in the world.

The demeaning of women throughout society is both subtle and blatant. It eats away at our self-esteem, holds us hostage and makes us fearful of giving our gifts. When women shrink back from life, the healing feminine energy and higher knowledge we bring, which are so needed to create peace and balance, go missing and things fall apart—in our households, our communities and the world.

We're living in societies that have lost their way and are driven by rich and powerful people seeking more of the same. Vulgarity rules. But just as our grands before us did, we can create a code of conduct that helps preserve us, use our power to protect women and children, and use our influence to help us love ourselves more and see ourselves as the champions we are.

We can tip our hats to what is fresh and fabulous without dishonoring God. We can celebrate our sexuality without being foul, or demeaning ourselves. We sisters and brothers can carry our own head! We rest on the shoulders of ancestors who struggled to give us the many choices we have today. We owe it to them not to assist in our own annihilation, but to determine that everything we do is in alignment with our purpose and reflects the beauty, creativity and nobility of our mighty race.

*Let us see ourselves, not through the filters of a sick society, but from a place connected to the rhythm of nature that values everything about being a woman and a Black woman, the first woman on Earth.*

# soul call

She's a well-known sister, at the top her profession and getting paid. Sis is creative in every way—in her own business and everyone else's. She's a "got-your-back" kind of girl and generous to a fault. I've seen her fly across the Atlantic at her own expense to help out a friend. She's all about solutions, as much a therapist as an artist. And Sis's personal style is the news. She mixes Prada and Tracy Reese with her grandmother's treasures and will top it off with a fur in any color. Her home is a showcase of the latest high-tech wizardry. It's all picture-perfect.

But Sis is talking suicide. Says she's done living with the pain of the sexual abuse and betrayal she suffered as a child. So I'm trying to find the best therapist for her issues. But getting her to go is like pulling teeth. She argues that she doesn't have the time—and doesn't think therapy will do her any good.

Then she asks me what I'm writing about in my next In the Spirit, suggesting that with her in my life there's much I could explore. And she's right: Her experience mirrors my own and maybe yours at times. We'll go over the top to take care of others and become a slave to the puffery popular culture says is the latest thing but give little attention to what's eating away at our insides.

A breath ago it was happening to me. I was in an emotional tangle—hot flashes, lost libido, crying jags, memory challenges. Thought I was losing my mind. But through it all I never missed a family commitment, a business meeting or a hair appointment. Only when pain was turning to panic did I stop to explore why I was feeling off-center and awful. I haven't mastered it yet, but I'm learning to integrate time for reflection, nurturing and healing into my everyday life, not just when I'm in a crisis.

We're all hungering so for love and connection, but searching for it outside ourselves shifts our attention to things that are secondary, tertiary or of no consequence at all. And so our looks and relationships, career and earnings—things that are ever-changing—become our sources of self-worth. We focus on making sure our package is wrapped tight and forget about the gift, the self inside.

What we don't claim, we can't honor.

Sis is finally sitting with a therapist each week and committing to doing what we must do in our life: She's taking inventory of what is working and not working for her interior world. She's untying the knots of anger, confusion, anxiety and false images of herself she believed in. She's doing the hard work of healing the self-blame and deeply rooted pain she has hosted from the violations she suffered as a child at the hands of her father and several other men.

One of the first things women must do to connect with our dignity and love is heal our relationship with our bodies. The message both women and men receive is that the female body exists for the pleasure of men. Boys must learn early on that sexual violence is an abuse of power and unjust. Boys must be taught that the female body is sacred, a celebration of our power to form bonds of communion and bring forth life, and that to oppress women in any way injures males too. It is self-violation as well and will haunt them, divorcing them from themselves and from God.

Healing is also possible with truth-telling, by acknowledging the violation and accountability. But as my young friend knows, forgiveness can be a long process.

All of us women carry with us the trauma of early experiences in relationship to our bodies. Too fat, too thin; too dark, too light; too tall, too short; not enough hair; breasts too big or too small; nose too wide; butt too fat or flat. So we try to adjust and turn ourselves into ornaments and models of desirability. It's our ritual, an ancient tradition. With the hours women put into getting glam, we could change the world.

We need the luster that comes with clarity, not a cover-up for emotional confusion. Let us see ourselves, our entire selves, throughout our life, not through the filters of a sick society but from a place connected to the rhythm of nature that values everything about being a woman and a Black woman—the first woman on earth.

Authentic beauty, changing with the seasons of our life, emanates from self-love and the knowledge that each of us is a divine original—spiritual, social and political—fashioned by God.

# notes

# Walk-on-Water Faith

*Life is a journey of exploration, risk, discovery and change, change, change. There are no sure maps to guide you, but your soul knows the way.*

# the divine design

Our life seldom moves forward in a straight line, or unfolds in the way we want it to. Life is like a giant jigsaw puzzle that mystifies us because there's no picture on a box top we can view to show us how all the many pieces fit together. But though the myriad shapes and sizes are scattered about, there is a Divine design, a perfect plan. We just can't see the whole picture—and we want it to be a pastoral scene.

The brilliant race man Frederick Douglass said it so well: "We want the bountiful rain but not the thunder, the treasures of the ocean but not its awful roar." The rain and the thunder, the treasures in the ocean and its roar—all these things are a part of life, and all that life serves up is necessary to the whole. All is good, all is God—just what we need to step up to greatness.

Life is an awesome, infinite process, always in a positive flow. The proof is all around us and within us. Look at our universe: trillions of stars, including our sun, spinning, spiraling, revolving in billions of galaxies—worlds colliding, dying, all in a perfect cosmic dance. The planets, the seasons, the flora and fauna, creatures great and small, your life and mine, always changing—and always according to the Divine Design. Nothing that God created is haphazard: You didn't stumble onto the planet! You were called for this hour. Your presence on Earth was preordained.

Our rational mind gets confused, makes us long for a life free of pain, challenge or change. But life is an adventure, a great journey of exploration, risk, discovery and change, change, change. There are no sure maps to guide you, but your destination is assured. Your soul knows the way. Our soul has come to Earth to refine itself, and it chose the divine right body needed to attend to the tasks God put before it. We are body, mind and soul—all of us in life's finishing school.

I was grabbing a bite to eat in the Indianapolis airport when a sister and I engaged in a conversation about these very things. I could see the fear and sadness in her eyes as she approached me to say hello. Sharon, a young single mother, was being forced out of a job she said she needed.

Like Sharon, we never know what we will encounter next: loss, betrayal, a health challenge, the transition of a loved one. And the solution to whatever challenge we face is always the same: not to give our power to panic; to stand firmly in the faith that we are forever in God's care. Regardless of appearances, the Divine Design is beneath what appears to be chaos, so lean not upon your own understanding. Know that when things fall apart, they only do so in order for God to give you something better, to make more for you.

Sharon admitted that she couldn't stand going to work each day, that she was undervalued, overworked and underpaid and had no opportunity for advancement after working at the company for nearly a decade. She had wanted out but lacked the courage to leave. Now the universe was answering her cry.

By the time we left each other to dash for our planes, Sharon could see that being pushed out was exactly what she needed. Now she could switch fields, as she had wanted to do. She could also negotiate a substantial severance package that would give her the lump sum she hadn't been able to save to make a down payment on a home.

God gives us unconditional love and support, and this will never change; everything else in our life will—our career, our body, relationships, all our circumstances. The game of life is won in remembering that God is our sure bet.

Listen to your intuition, not your fears. Sharon was forced to merge her talents with her life goals. The last time we spoke she had become a real estate broker, had purchased her second rental property and was doing swell.

The sole purpose of our journey is to learn that "You are gods." To live in the full strength of your being, you only have to show up, loving, working your plan and trusting the Divine Design as it unfolds.

*Stop the whirl and lay your body down in silence each day. The in-between time calls for more God listening, more soul work and greater faith.*

# blessed assurance

Call it zeitgeist—the spirit of the time. Everywhere people are in transition, trying to create a better life. We're longing for peace and balance, for pure joy. And we want deep healing that reaches beyond ourselves to "right-doing" in our country and in our world. We know that neither corporations nor the government is up to it. And that science won't end hunger, poverty or war. We are our own salvation. We are the healers we've been waiting for; we are the leaders, the ones who can set things right. The anxiety we feel is divine discontent. It is God's call to us to heal ourselves, our community and Mother Earth.

Our personal world—along with our larger one—mirrors our beliefs and behavior. Ignorance is the source of our pain, the saboteur that leads us to violate spiritual laws. And when we break them, we pay for it. God puts us through the paces, giving us the difficult lessons we need and should find difficult to ignore.

The practice that maintains our individual health and equilibrium applies to the larger society as well. In a word, it's charity. My mother, Babs, seemed to say it every day: "Charity begins at home and spreads abroad." Serve yourself or suffer. Serve one another or die.

It's astonishing that we whine and complain so much—about our children in underserved schools, that prisons are the new plantations, about how hard we work, how tired we are, and how we've been disappointed, abandoned, abused. If we think our personal and political challenges are great, then we don't know our history. We've forgotten what the generations before ours endured so we could be.

The dreams of yesterday's Black folks weren't for themselves; they were for us. The brilliant scholar and minister Dr. Renita Weems reminds us that if you are anybody, it's because some Black person stooped low enough to let you climb on and ride piggyback into the future.

We are the people who refused to die. Look back at what your elders went through, remember what our ancestors endured, and you gain the clarity and courage to create the magnificent tomorrow God wants for you. Half a millennium of oppression may have diminished our confidence and self-esteem, but not the love, growth and support God guarantees.

Spirit is waiting for you, within you. Do what your forebears did—don't yield. Press on. Focus on what they knew—that God is the ability beyond our ability. This is how they got over.

The in-between time calls for more God listening, more soul work and greater faith. Stop the whirl and lay your body down in silence each day. Close your eyes and listen to your slow, deep, rhythmic breathing—it is the activity of God within you. Be with it, stay with it. Feel the fear or whatever you're going through. But don't own it, because it's not yours to bear. Take a leap of faith and give the weight to God. Live the legacy. Plan, work and trust. Whisper this: Thy will be done. I give myself to you.

No matter how the landscape appears, God never fails. We are here, survivors and thrivers—living, breathing proof.

*When something is meant for you, it can never be
lost or taken away. And when it's not for you, it simply
won't come your way—and that's a blessing, too.*

# thy will be done

Our lives don't lie. Our joys, sorrows, challenges and triumphs reflect our deep, often unconscious beliefs, just as the choices we have made mirror where we are on our journey.

If your experience is like mine, your most difficult moments have come from resisting change. We hold on to what's familiar, even when it's hurting us. We stay in unhealthy relationships rather than learning to love and cherish ourselves and our own good company. We may resist doing the work to heal our addictions even when they're destroying our physical and emotional well-being. At times we resent our circumstances, forgetting that whatever they are, we are still in life's positive flow. We feel alone, though we are never alone—and afraid, though we have nothing to fear. The moment we remember Spirit's guiding love within and around us, our pressures begin to ease.

To humble yourself and surrender to God—this is life's great spiritual challenge. Yes, we need vision and passion, need to be engaged in life, planning, creating, re-creating, but we have to consciously let go of our attachment to the outcome. God asks us to entrust the details of our lives, the timing of our every blessing, to a Wisdom that is greater than we are and to find the sacred in our every circumstance.

Whew!!! That's so hard. But when something is meant for you, it can never be lost or taken away. If it's not for you, it simply won't come your way, and that's a blessing, too. The task is to stay positive and focused on the big picture, so you will see along the path the treasures, ever plentiful, that God has laid out just for you—everything you need to fulfill yourself and your life's purpose.

Faith. Sweet surrender. Trusting in the goodness of life. Understanding that everything, everyone has a reason and season for being. Allowing folks to be who they are and things to unfold in divine order, rather than criticizing, worrying, stressing, trying to force them to work our way. This is the source of inner peace, the path of joy and infinite possibilities. When I'm challenged, I hold those thoughts in my heart and this one in my mind: I can't wait to see how God's going to work this one out, and the good that will come from it.

Sweet surrender is born of the faith that we're always in God's care. We have only to ask God to ease, order and organize our lives, to stand for us when we feel weak. This is how I stopped smoking years ago; how I stopped sweating my mother's every criticism; how I let go of a man I loved who wasn't healthy enough to love me well. It's how I found the courage to do work that demanded talent and skill greater than I thought I had.

I love and want to live Jamaican writer and poet Jean Wilson's powerful words: "No more smalling up of me."

Surrender to God your every burden—fear, guilt, anger, illness, addictions, financial woes—everything holding you back. Banish "can't" from your vocabulary. Sweet surrender, faith, leaves no room for doubt or fear. It's the ultimate paradox: What you fight, you strengthen. To be strong in the world, you have to be patient, humble and willing to let go. The spiritual warrior's path is one of complete nonresistance, sweet surrender. Surrender the illusion of control, and you relax into your great spiritual power. Bow to the Source with absolute faith, just as our foreparents did.

Embrace the gifts of grace and divine protection that are yours; they were bestowed on you at birth. And practice living each day by the most powerful words ever spoken: Thy will be done.

*No matter how bad things appear, God is always preparing you*
*for something better. The Holy Spirit breaks down the old to*
*make room for what is shining and new and coming to you.*

# give it to God

Are you hooked on worry? For most of us, worry is as familiar as daylight. We all have our personal woes. And these days the nightly news is not so good. Our worries compound, and they add up to frustration, stagnation and anxiety that cut deep into our life. The result of all this stress and strain is no secret: It makes us sick.

It has been proven that anxious people have more accidents, eat and drink more, medicate themselves more, and suffer more strokes and heart attacks. A beloved friend is winning a war with a serious illness, but says she's now clear about why she's having to do battle: "Stress!" she says. "All last year I wore myself down worrying about things I hardly remember, things that don't matter now." Stress makes us vulnerable. Anxiety doubles our trouble.

But unlearning is possible. You can control what you think: Free will is God's greatest gift to us. Our thinking is the basis of all our difficulties—it's at the heart of our insecurities and of problems in our relationships, the root cause of every conflict in the world. If we want a new and better life, our thinking has to be new and better. If we want a new and better world, our leadership has to be different.

Worry is negative energy that blocks insight and inspiration and blinds us to the evidence of God's endless giving. Our minds, not the world, have run amok. In this seeing-is-believing culture, it's difficult to perceive the perfection in all things or to see that the universe is always working on our behalf.

Hold on to this truth and bring a sense of adventure, not worry, to navigating your life's twists and turns. No matter how bad things appear, God is always preparing you for something better. The Holy Spirit breaks down the old to make room for what's new and different that's coming your way. How many times have you lost faith or thought you'd lost your way simply because you couldn't see the hand of God at work?

Stop worry in its tracks. Try it right now. Engage your will, your most powerful tool, to stop worrying about what's next. Tell your mind it will focus only on solutions, that you will permit only faith, not fear, and that all your thoughts will flow in one direction: toward the goodness of God. Begin practicing today with little difficulties, and in time you will easily work through the bigger issues. Give up the stubborn notion that your life has got to follow your script for you to be happy. Then you won't be disappointed or anxious when situations unfold differently—and you'll see they even unfold in a better way than you'd hoped or asked for.

When you face challenges, trust God to do what God does all day, every day: fix things.

*The ritual of journaling is liberating and healing.*
*It grounds us in our own wisdom and clarity that*
*emerge when we open our heart and put pen to paper.*

# notes from the heart

When I was a child, I kept a diary, a little blue book with a lock and key that Goddie, my brother's godmother and Mommy's best friend, had given me on my eighth birthday. I'd sit quietly some evenings in my family's tiny apartment and write about my escapades in school and on the few blocks I navigated each day in my bustling Harlem neighborhood.

By the time I was a teenager I had moved with my family to Queens, an outer borough of New York City, leaving behind my friends and everything that was familiar. But through my little diary I could stay in touch with a self and with experiences I never wanted to forget. What joy I would feel over the years reading the large curly script that recounted my days and described the things that mattered to me.

As I grew older I often felt the need to write about my life—not just to record the happenings of the day, as I had done as a child, but also to explore the events in my life, what I was "growing through" and feeling deeply. Despite the need, I rarely allowed myself that important ritual, because I feared that my mother, and later on my daughter, would discover the secrets I wanted to keep.

Today I appreciate what the beloved poet and essayist Audre Lorde tried to convince me of just before she passed away. I was in St. Croix, spending the afternoon visiting Audre and her partner, Dr. Gloria Joseph. Audre, who left us a rich body of personal writings that give any reader courage and strength, spoke to me in that soft and certain way she had about the importance of keeping a journal and writing in it each day. "There are powers and rewards in self-conscious living," our sage sister said. And though I haven't kept a formal journal that I write in every day, throughout the past decade I have taken notes on my life.

We may not always be comfortable sharing our deepest feelings with others, but we'd better know what they are. If we aren't open to our own deepest truths, how will we know what we are seeking? As the intimate and personal writings of brave sisters like Audre Lorde, Maya Angelou, bell hooks and Alice Walker attest, one of the first steps toward wholeness is telling the truth to yourself, opening your heart to yourself so that you gain clarity about what is true for you. Writing from your heart helps you discover the depth of your soul.

Sharing our intimacies is not only healing to us, but helps others as well to understand that we need not be victims of the past. There's no more powerful example of this than our young sisters Ayana Byrd and Akiba Solomon's stunningly candid anthology *Naked*, in which Black women write boldly and candidly about sexuality, their bodies and beauty.

Asali Solomon, an English professor and Akiba's sister, says this in her essay "Fuzzy Black Thing":

> *Tell yourself what you will. Everyone knows that the most valuable capital that a woman can possess is a beauty that other people agree on. But many women have to decide that they are beautiful in spite of what they've been told by high school boys, employers, and music videos. I did. I'm medium-height, dark-skinned, and thick around the middle, with flat, size nine, corn-flecked feet. I know I'm beautiful because I decided that this is the case. But sometimes I can't shake the sinking feeling that no one besides my parents and sister know it.*

*With apologies to DuBois, I've raced past modern double con-*
*sciousness right into the collective mental illness of postmodern mul-*
*ticonsciousness. I can see myself through the eyes of the brother in*
*the obscenely shiny black Escalade who stares right through me, the*
*White woman smiling at me curiously in the supermarket, and the*
*Mexican construction worker who leers at me with erotic hostility.*
*Despite how I try to see myself, it sometimes catches me and takes*
*my breath away that for the most part I'm homely because I'm*
*brown and nappy.*

We needn't possess the poetic voice of the professor or of Toni Morrison or Audre Lorde to document the truth of our experience. We should just preserve for ourselves our thoughts, feelings and experiences, however they flow. The ritual of writing, journaling, isn't about spelling, grammar or syntax; it's about liberation and healing. It grounds us in our own wisdom and clarity that emerge when we open our heart and put pen to paper. Writing from our heart, we get behind the labels others may have put on us and the disguises we wear. We resolve the issues in our past and discover our truth.

As we document our lives, we begin to see patterns and connections, and develop an awareness of the things that cause us pain and suffering and those that increase our happiness and joy. In time we become more aware of how the choices we make create our experiences, why we were happy and hopeful in April and down in the dumps in May.

The wisdom that prompted Goddie's gift and Audre's words helps us live more from inner guidance. Writing about our life encourages us to be conscious of the journey and to see the distance we have traveled.

*Three hours a day of mindless TV watching equals six weeks of 24-hour days wasted each year. The challenge is not to learn how to do more, but rather to stop majoring in minor things.*

# a continuing journey

We were high up in the mountains that glorious weekend at the Betty Shabazz Wholistic Retreat Center at Kings Lodge in Otisville, New York. About 60 of us sisters and brothers from all over the country—writers and aspiring scribes—had gathered at the Black Writers Retreat. And this was the session no one wanted to miss: the workshop by Amiri Baraka, poet, professor, social critic and iconoclast. Baraka inspired, tested, teased and chastened us with a long list of great literary works by James Baldwin, Aimé Césaire, W.E.B. DuBois, Buchi Emecheta, Langston Hughes, Lorraine Hansberry, Zora Neale Hurston and others whose books are must-reads for all Black folks who want to be conscious and literate.

Too often I chastise myself for not having certain skills and information, then pressure myself to acquire them instantly. So my first inclination was to rush out, gather the books and dive into them, several at a time. But that approach has never worked. I knew that within weeks the books would be swept aside by the next wave of urgent projects.

Growth and development take time and are a never-ending journey. God's not rushing us or requiring that we be superhuman, so why put that pressure on ourselves?

The challenge is not to learn how to do more, but rather to stop majoring in minor things. Three hours a day of mindless TV watching equals six weeks of 24-hour days wasted each year. We have to eliminate the things that don't serve us in any meaningful way so we can free up time for what is nourishing and fulfilling. There'll be no room in our life for the feast until we clear our platter of junk food.

Say your goal is to get fit and focused and boost your energy. You pledge to exercise, meditate, drink eight glasses of water and eat nourishing food every day. But just as I won't become an instant literary scholar, no snacks-eating couch potato turns into a health-conscious force of nature overnight.

A new plan has a better chance of becoming a way of life when introduced in stages. You'll more likely stay with a fitness regimen if you start by taking a 20-minute walk three times a week and drinking one more glass of water each day, then add ten minutes of deep breathing, then replace a breakfast donut with a protein drink. Remember the Rule of 21: Do anything consistently for 21 days and it becomes a habit.

A journey of a thousand miles begins with a single step. As our steps grow bolder and more confident, we build momentum, and in time we become unstoppable. We have infinite power to change, to make our lives over if we choose. But we have to be disciplined, courageous and patient. We have to persevere and be ruthless about valuing and managing our time.

I'm going to savor reading our important literature, one book at a time, by forgoing activities that are less meaningful to me.

Choose with great care what you want for your life. Be patient and passionate, and have a plan. Then put your power and energy behind that intention and keep striving, keep working to bring it to fruition.

*Perfection isn't a requirement or even a possibility*
*for us human beings; only love and sincerity are.*
*This is a lesson we were born to learn.*

# imitation of life

I wouldn't have a friend who's as critical of me as I am of myself. Like most folks, I want to be perfect, and when I feel less than that, my chattering mind berates me: *You should have balanced work and motherhood better and spent more quality time with Shana when she was growing up. . . . Just look at your desk—clutter, chaos, papers everywhere. You must be losing your mind. . . . That was a really foolish thing you said at yesterday's meeting. . .* Pick, pick, pick.

I look at you, my beloved, and see myself: overscheduled, overworked, anxious, yet believing I should do and be more. My friend Terrie has built a major business from scratch and authored several books; she lectures nationwide and mentors dozens of kids. But she feels down most days because of her weight. And Pat—who has raised two children on her own and put them through college, who cares for her mother and extended family—beats up on herself because her business hasn't grown as quickly as she hoped it would.

We grow up believing we must be smart, kind, organized, disciplined, successful, witty and unruffled—perfect. And there are the punishing messages we women internalize about our bodies: You will be accepted or rejected based on your looks.

We learn to reject pieces of ourselves early on, taking our cue from critical adults and the images in media we unconsciously absorb. But finding our definition through the eyes of others, who may be more confused than we are, is playacting. It's imitating life, not living it. We will never achieve the ideal because it's false, an illusion created with smoke and mirrors—lights, cameras, photo retouching. Our desire for perfection is our worst enemy if we don't distinguish between our individual quirks and truly harmful behavior, the issues our spirit came to the physical plane to work out.

We don't have to be perfect to love ourselves. God alone is perfect. Perfection isn't a requirement or even a possibility for us human beings; only love and sincerity are. No doubt this is a lesson I was born to learn.

Wherever we find ourselves along the path at this moment is a necessary step in our development. Our challenge is to know ourselves and to appreciate who we are just as we are. This is the foundation of deep self-confidence. When we look outward for meaning and validity, we stumble because we are out of step with the Divine Guidance that turns sun and earth and breathes in us. Consider the lilies of the field. . . . Walt Whitman put it this way:

> I exist as I am, that is enough.
> If no other in the world be aware I sit content,
> And if each and all be aware I sit content.
> One world is aware, and by far the largest to me,
> and that is myself.
> And whether I come to my own today or in
> ten thousand
> or ten million years,
> I can cheerfully take it now, or with equal cheerfulness,
> I can wait.

# the power of thought

Imagine what your life would be if you were free of doubt, free of feelings of insecurity. Endless possibilities would be yours to explore, unhampered by limited thinking and anxiety over your shortcomings. You would see your magnificence. This is proven all around us: We need to see what we want in order to create it. We need to say what we want in order to have it.

Long before Iyanla Vanzant became a household name, she was a master in the spiritual realm. Years ago she told me she was planning for her forthcoming book to be on the *New York Times* Best Sellers List. Iyanla wrote her name and book title on the list, clipped it from the paper, and tacked it to her office wall. This no doubt heightened her passion for the work she was creating and reminded her each day that the rewards of striving for excellence would be hers. That phenomenal book, *In the Meantime*, did make the *Times* Best Sellers List and remained there for 18 months.

For every blessing we receive, some corner of our mind is whispering: *This is what I want and I can have it.* Deep desire and a welcoming heart open roads for grace to travel toward us. Our negative thoughts have equal power to block the way.

So how do our thoughts materialize? Thought is "truly powerful, truly magic and capable of manifesting itself in all its fullness," explained the renowned Bulgarian mystic Omraam Mikhaël Aïvanhov. Born in 1900 and teaching in France in the 1930's, he posited that thoughts are "recorded":

They put lines of communication in place on the astral level. "From there to the material gesture," said Aïvanhov, "is only a short step."

Our human vocabulary is limited in explaining our divine nature. Our mind is of God, and its ability to envision and make manifest is a power beyond the comprehension of our intellect. Using this gift purposefully, we tap into a higher dimension of intelligence.

Peeling away the layers of negativity and disbelief takes time and vigilance. Be present to yourself. Know what's going on in your mind: what you're feeling during a meeting, while working at your desk, driving, shopping, washing dishes. Make it your habit to glance inward and check on your thoughts and feelings—for here is your true command center. This is where the flight or the fall is arranged. What we think and envision today is creating our tomorrow. See and expect the positive, and you will advance your own evolution and contribute tremendously to transforming life on earth.

Humanity is a seeing tribe; we are hardwired to use the unique power of imagination. Envision what you want: Focus deliberately on solutions and host only happy, wholesome thoughts. Joining God in the creative act, you will call forth love and positive experiences.

*Set your sights high. Raise the bar and follow your dreams. The Holy Spirit put them into your heart for you to pursue. With faith and action behind them, the universe will organize its resources around your intention.*

# life without limits

So many of us sisters are on a mission to recover the parts of ourselves we feel we've lost. We want to reclaim our power, our passion, our purpose and, most of all, our joy. At times we find ourselves searching and sifting for the internal authority we acted on so easily as girls. We want to find again the dreams we seem to have laid aside, and feel the sureness of our earlier conviction.

Society's fear of feminine power, its devaluation of women's contributions, and its dismissal of our voices still take a toll on our confidence and self-esteem. Through social policies and in popular culture, in the workplace and often in our homes we are treated with condescension and made to feel inferior. In some way this has hurt all women. And not just women: The world is in chaos, out of balance, in part because nothing can work well when half of humanity lives at half measure. But sisters are moving toward a spiritual rebirth.

Pregnant with intelligence and intuition, creativity and the compassion of our sacred heart, we long to bring love and peace to our life, concord to our communities, and justice to society. We know the consequences will be terrible if we don't, and we know that the work we are to do in the world must be born within us. Giving birth to a new self, as in childbirth, is painful and messy. At times we feel afraid. New ideas and ways of being shake things up. But the legacy that will carry our name is worth the pain of opening up to our Higher Self. Resisting life—not being who you are, not living what you know— is far more painful.

As poet Audre Lorde asked, "How can we build a nation if we're afraid to speak out, afraid to walk out into the moonlight?"

Fear restricts the flow of life. It makes us depressed and ill. Fear veils clarity and can cause a woman to forget herself in intimate relationships. Faith is the counterbalance to fear.

We Black women talk a lot about faith, and now we must act on it. Imagine the life you want—one far beyond the bounds prescribed by custom, which says that just getting by is good enough. Our soul seeks peace, balance and authentic self-expression. It pushes us to reevaluate our dreams and desires, our power and potential—urges us to step off the treadmill and into a magnificent, soul-satisfying life and a sane society of our own creation.

What is your divine assignment? What have you come to learn, develop and give back to life? What is your big idea? Set your sights high. Raise the bar and follow your dream. The Holy Spirit put it into your heart for you to pursue. Put faith and action behind it, and the universe will organize its resources around your intention. All that you need begins with you. All that our people need begins with us.

The life we want awaits us. It's time for us to rise, shake off the dust of limited thinking, and with bold authority step into the light.

*Move out of the world of measurement and judgment, and your life gets easier. You expect no harm from change. You simply part like a river around a rock, continuing toward the sea.*

# keep your hands wide open

My friend Peggy Ruffin is so defined by her open heart. She sees beauty everywhere and pauses to appreciate it. Whether at a 'round-the-way dive or a high-brow capital-city gathering, Peggy has never met a stranger. We all are drawn to her gentle spirit, her joy and integrity, her comfort with herself. She doesn't need her hair, her home, her life to be in order to invite you in. Even when she's pressed for time, Peg's not rushing and won't hurry you. We've been friends since grade school, and what I cherish most about my girl is that you can tell her anything—about something you're deeply ashamed of, the worst thing you ever did—and she won't judge you. She's had her share of loss and heartache, but Peggy doesn't play the blame game. She knows it's all a gift, the raw material for creating a better life.

Abbey Lincoln wrote so profoundly and sings so passionately: "Give your love, live your life, each and every day. And keep your hands wide open, and let the sun shine through, 'cause you can never lose a thing if it belongs to you."

Stress and anxiety evaporate as we loosen our grip. Letting go isn't giving up. It's only giving up trying to change people and control what you can't: the unseen Force that strings together this thing called life.

Harshly judging ourselves and one another and trying to control every outcome has made Black women weary and harmed our relationships. Let's soften our hearts in all our interactions, especially toward people who irritate us the most. Sisters and brothers need to cut one another some slack instead of tearing down our own house. Instead let's start tearing down the fences that separate us so we can work and build together.

Our hardest work is going beyond our learned behavior, and healing ourselves so that we finally stop passing our pain and dysfunction from one generation to the next. To the degree that I like myself for who I really am and stop finding fault with what God made, I break out of a self-constructed prison. How we feel about ourselves is reflected in how we treat everyone else and how creatively we use whatever life sends us.

For a bit of time today, notice how easily you judge yourself, others and each event. Notice how tight and grim you feel. Then take a few deep breaths, relax and decide to have a love affair with life, making no negative judgments about anyone or anything. Go with the flow and feel the difference.

As we move out of the world of measurement and judgment, we trust in divine order more, and life gets easier. We love ourselves more and find a new kinship with others. We are kinder, more appreciative and healthier too. We expect no harm from change, from the natural flow of life, which we can never direct. Like Peggy, we simply part like a river around a rock, continuing toward the sea.

# notes

Temple of the Body

*Saying no takes courage. Saying no can be life-affirming; it makes a place for peace, health and happiness to take root in us. Creating well-being and balance requires letting go before adding on.*

# give yourself the blessing

I'm finally getting it right. I'm answering the call to rearrange my life so that it gives me more freedom and fulfillment. I see clearly now that whether we're after personal, professional or spiritual growth, the wisdom is the same: Be truthful and clear about where you are in your life; ferret out the philosophies and strategies to take you where you want to go, then practice them.

Role models are up close and personal in my world. The folks living soul-satisfying lives—whether they're business or community leaders or heading up happy, loving families—have their priorities straight. They don't work harder than others; they're just smarter about focusing their energies, setting goals and boundaries, and not allowing what matters most to be at the mercy of what matters least.

Creating a life that's rich and satisfying requires letting go before adding on. We need to begin asking ourselves what not to do. Saying no takes courage. Saying no can be life-affirming. Saying no can clear the way. Excuse yourself from phone conversations that are about nothing, and hours open up in your day. Avoid the bag of chips, and your heart, blood pressure and hips offer appreciation. Turn off the TV, go to sleep and rise early for quiet time with God, and your spirit soars.

Too many people I know are succumbing to stress and illness. They are dying out of season. A longtime friend is overworked and overwhelmed—and so depressed about it she needs her meds to get out of bed and go to work. A brother I love, years my junior, is battling prostate cancer and has had two heart attacks. Managing illness distracts and exhausts us and robs us of the attention and strengths that should be used to celebrate the feast of life. Stress, depression, obesity, addiction, hypertension, diabetes, kidney disease: Aren't illnesses sapping the energy and creativity of too many people in your world?

It could happen to us. And it does happen when we don't make space in our life for ourselves, a place for peace, health and happiness to become our highest priorities. Nothing matters more.

We can work our way back into balance. We can draw upon a wealth of therapies and the gifts of nature to heal both the inner and outer rhythm of our life. We hold the keys to those powers. We alone can give or deny ourselves the exquisite pleasure of savoring our life. I know this, yet at times my crazy-busy life causes me to lose my connection with the natural rhythm of life, with its ebb and flow, give and take, seed and flower.

But life always gives us a wake-up call and proves to us that we can't break its laws and thrive. Saying yes to self-preservation is our first divine duty. We have to be here to give our warmth, softness and love, the only gifts that really matter.

Not everyone in my world is happy when I say, "So sorry. . . . Can't do it, Suga'. . . . Not available." What's new is that saying no doesn't worry me. I'm freeing time to be with me. For deeper thinking, more joy and laughter—all greatly needed for good health and equilibrium. I'm giving the engine some rest.

Lose what's unnecessary. Give yourself the blessing of the space you will create. Clear a place, plant the seed, help it grow. Then celebrate the harvest.

*My friend Angela now says cancer was the best thing that ever happened to her, that it entered her life like the spirit of truth and transformed her negativity, her resistance to change and self-caring.*

# make room for your life

The gorgeous month of September in the Northeast always awakens in me a need for reflection. Summer's end tells me it's time to pause, to meet myself in a quiet place and rethink my purpose and priorities. It's as if my spiritual calendar is calling me toward clarity and renewal before the frenzied holidays ahead, coaxing me to deepen and strengthen my relationship with God as the autumn winds begin to blow.

I'm beginning to live more fully what I've known for years: Smart women and men heed the whispering of their body and soul before it becomes a scream. My friend Angela Trafford, a breast-cancer survivor, admits she only heard the holler, "the voice of my illness," after a second bout with the deadly disease. But Angela now says cancer was the best thing that ever happened to her, that it entered her life like the spirit of truth and transformed her negativity, her resistance to change and self-caring.

Let's be wise enough to make a ritual of replenishing what daily living depletes so illness won't force us to lay our body down.

Our culture hasn't taught us to heed the need for downtime. Feeling stressed, anxious and ill have become accepted ways of living for us. We learn early on that we're born to work, to sacrifice and serve others, that focusing on our own needs is selfish.

Today our lives are complex, overscheduled and harried. We're all living in the high-stress zone—and paying a high emotional and physical price for it. We've learned to suffer in silence—especially Black women. We are expert at looking good while feeling bad.

Take back your power and your life, and make no excuses! Much of our stress is self-imposed. I see now that I'll never finish all the work. I'll never be able to answer all the calls and e-mails, or complete all the to-dos—so I've stopped killing myself trying.

Set your priorities, and every day do something to unclutter and uncomplicate your life. Now, before the rush of the holidays, weed out the things you don't use or need and the negative folks who make you weary. Simplify your outer world and make room for your life.

Just 15 minutes of quiet time each day will refresh and restore you. It will wash away the stress and the blocks to your awareness of God's presence within you.

Surround yourself with your favorite candles and flowers. Sit still, close your eyes, slow and deepen your breathing. Give thanks for the bountiful blessings all around you, for Mother Earth's generous and reliable support. Have your quiet talk with the Master. God knows all your needs. Listen in the silence and you will hear the Holy Spirit's answers. God will order your steps; you will know God's will for you.

Create the space and Spirit will speak to you there, offering wisdom and peace. Remember and draw upon that understanding throughout the day. When Baby Brother acts crazy, when someone annoys you, don't react. Don't go there. Put your highest self in charge; remember the One.

It's just this simple: Pause, take a few deep breaths, and you will see clearly that no matter what appears to be going on in the outer world, God's perfect peace is within you. Wherever you are, you are standing on holy ground.

*We are perfect, awe-inspiring miracle machines. As we move closer to the blueprint God created for each of us, we become healthier, happier, stronger and more energized.*

# get lifted

Four numbers note the year of our birth. In time, four more will note the year of our death. The dash between indicates the space where our life is lived. With that final number, our life will be etched in stone, immutable. But at this moment, life is clay in our creative hands. We can shape it any way we choose. How will you mold this divine clay during the rest of that mad dash that is your life?

There is no more important question to think about as the winds of change are blowing. Women throughout the world are becoming a mightier force. This is God's plan. Futurist Nat Irvin II says that Black women will change forever our communities and countries. "The wind is at your back," he declares. So take courage and fly, lift your eyes, and aim toward the sky. Don't let fear or anyone's negativity or doubt drain your energy, weigh you down, or cause you to veer from your high calling.

In the life God wants for you, there's no room for ailments that weigh heavily on the body and soul and keep you from soaring. We are awe-inspiring miracle machines. No matter what is aching or ailing us, mentally or physically, we are not planted there. Every painful emotion, every throb or sting tells us where we are, where we're headed. As we move closer to the blueprint God created for each of us, we become happier, stronger and more energized. As we move away, we grow uneasy, unhappy, ill. Pain is the indicator, the encouragement to get on course. Perfect harmony is the law governing the universe and all that God created. We human beings are given a special blessing—dominion over ourselves, a marriage of creative energy and free will. But this blessing also means we can break nature's law and cause chaos and suffering.

Are you in law-breaking mode?

The ongoing work of life is to continually reorder our days to support our dreams and the calling that God put in our heart.

I was in law-breaking mode recently and got a wake-up call when my hip started to ache. A specialist recommended either steroid injections every few months or surgery. Now I notice physically challenged people everywhere, both younger and older than I, using canes and wheelchairs, pushing walkers.

Oh, hell no! That's not the future I want. My hurting hip was the jolt I needed to do what I must to keep myself away from the surgeon's knife, from chronic pain, from getting stuck in illness and immobility. I've recommitted myself to regular exercise, to moving my body and life toward God's optimal blueprint for me.

Praise every effort you make to improve your life, and don't criticize yourself when you miss the mark.

Here are powerful affirmations to say each day:

• I claim my health and happiness right now.

• I claim fulfillment and mutual joy in all of my relationships right now.

• I am prepared to prosper and joyfully share my bounty right now.

We Black folks have to get up. We have work to do, and within each of us is a compass that directs us. Protecting and preserving your health is your job. No one but you can keep your life lifted and fulfilled. Restoring the spirit and health of the Black community is our village project. We are the physicians our people are hoping will soon arrive.

Visionary writer Alice Walker said it so well: Anything we love can be healed.

*Fitness is preventive medicine, testify our energetic elders in their eighties and at ninety. We can chase away obesity, hypertension, heart disease, diabetes, stroke—before they turn our life upside down.*

# from the wisdom front

Lettice Graham learned to swim at the merry age of 64. "I swim five days a week," the muscular and joyful 82-year-old tells me, looking exquisite in a fitted purple pantsuit, her silver locks dancing round her smile. "And I practice my yoga every morning," she adds. Hilda Stephenson, 90, won't miss her morning aerobics class and often walks miles, as does her 69-year-old daughter, Beverly Taylor. Morjorie Newlin, who works out four days a week, began a fitness regimen to improve her health at 72; today, at 83, she's winning bodybuilding competitions around the country and says, "I feel good every day."

These reports come from the wisdom front, from extraordinary women living this truth: Fitness is preventive medicine. Along with the other amazing women (and men) of every age in an *Essence* book, *Wisdom of the Ages*, these resilient women have succeeded in counteracting the deadly effects of obesity, which is epidemic among Black women, triggering a host of preventable diseases that are killing us.

High blood pressure, heart disease, diabetes, stroke—my own family history is riddled with these weight-related illnesses hitting our community hard. The weight-disease connection is real, but there is a deeper discomfort that's making us fat and ill: stress. Stress fires up the appetite and turns our lives upside down.

When under stress, the body in its natural wisdom releases cortisol, a fight-or-flight hormone, to assist in the emergency. Cortisol makes us crave quick-energy-producing sugary and starchy food. With chronic stress, it stays elevated so we feel hungry all the time. It also creates a biochemical imbalance, weakening the immune system and causing anxiety, depression, memory and learning difficulties, loss of libido and a host of gynecological problems.

Life speaks loudly to us sisters. And pain is information. Listen to what it is saying to you. God calls us to regain control of the sources of imbalance. Answering the call is critical to us and the future of our people. If Black women aren't well, our families and community won't thrive.

There is no shortcut to wellness. We must return to the Source and reconnect with what's right and true for us. Quiet time in prayer, meditation or journaling will give us a needed fresh start.

When you listen to the voice within, a transformative process begins. You learn to love yourself deeply. Your feeling of self-worth grows, along with the wisdom to release what drains you and adopt what nourishes you— without apology or fear of consequences. You'll value following a nutritional and fitness program that harmonizes body and soul.

As the wise elders in our book testify, it is never too late to learn to love what is good for you.

My wise guide Eric Butterworth would often quote from the poet Goethe: "Whatever you can do or dream, begin it/Boldness has genius, power and magic in it."

# notes

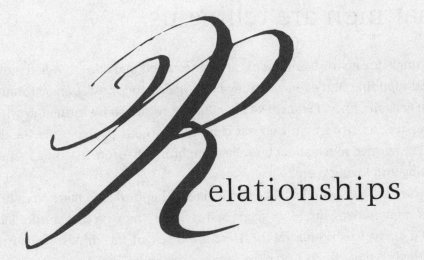

**R**elationships

*Carrying a list of complaints doesn't make us welcome company; and it kills intimacy and joy. Our partners are growing in their own way and in their own time, not ours.*

# what men are telling us

I was single for nearly twenty years after a troubled marriage that had moved beyond mending. But even when my heart ached the most, I knew I wanted to marry again, knew I wanted to be in harmony and share intimately with a progressive, sensitive man who was committed to our people. Over the decades, I've learned much about brothers from brothers—from listening to them, watching and loving them.

Now I have a second chance at marriage. Khephra and I married in 1989. He's compassionate and kind, smart and reliable, the type of beautiful Black man I'd said I was preparing for. Here are a few of the things I've learned about loving that, when I practice them successfully, make my relationship with my Khephie, and with myself, so much sweeter.

**Reserve a space for yourself.** Do what keeps you happy, healthy and fulfilled. Practicing self-love is the cardinal rule for making our partnerships whole. It gives us our own approval; it takes the pressure off our relationships. Otherwise our need for love is a bottomless pit that can never be filled by another.

**Be his lover, not his mother.** No one wants to be constantly "improved." Carrying a list of complaints doesn't make us welcome company, and it kills intimacy and joy. He's growing in his own way and in his own time, not yours.

**Resist the impulse to punish him for the past.** He cheated, he lied, he hurt you; or you're punishing him for the grief caused by an ex-lover. Truth is, we all mess up. We all need to be forgiven. We all have some forgiving to do. Learn to live and love in the present; let go of the past. And never raise the issue again.

**Tell him what you feel and what you want, kindly and directly.** Don't hint at it or be manipulative. Men can't read our minds. If you want him to take more responsibility for the children or give you a back rub, say so. Brothers need to hear from us more honestly and lovingly. This helps them trust enough to open their hearts.

**Don't correct him in front of others.** We all want to be right, and too often about things of no consequence. Who cares if Aunt Gussy visited in '04 or '06? Be unrelenting when it counts—say, in choosing the best family doctor and schools for the kids. Otherwise, choose to be happy.

**Be calm, be cool.** Turn down the volume in your intimate space and save fighting words for the liberation of our people.

**Let him be in his silence.** Each of us processes stuff differently. Don't attempt to enmesh yourself in his issues or invade his private space. His rhythm and needs are different from yours; respect them. And when he's silent, it doesn't mean something is wrong with you or him. Be your own source of joy, and before long he'll want to join you there.

**Bring on the romance.** Brothers say romance is not their responsibility alone. They won't resist candlelight dinners and evenings without the kids, and passionate sex.

All our personal relationships are calling us to take a softer, more loving stance with ourselves and one another. And when it comes to relationships, men are saying they want less drama and the consistent, compassionate and patient love we sisters, too, are longing for. Let's lead the way.

*You can survive anything but self-negation. Tolerate*
*abuse and you give up your sense of worth. And what*
*isn't good for you isn't good for anyone else—it isn't love.*

# love him or leave him

There's a sadness about couples whose love for each other is buried beneath anger and resentment. I know the hurt they feel because I've lived in that painful place myself, but never for long. There's nothing more wounding to our self-esteem and spirit than the melancholy we feel when we stay in a relationship that's turned bitter.

My parents stayed together without satisfaction. They learned to live in loneliness, without tenderness or intimacy. Babs and Lawrence didn't even have a "good-enough" marriage; despite its longevity—some 32 years—it was a failed marriage. Like so many couples, Babs and Lawrence maintained their unhappy union because they wanted stable lives for their children, and financially they couldn't afford to live apart. And though I'll be eternally grateful to my parents for sacrificing what I wouldn't, the bitterness between them hardened their hearts and soured any joy in our home. But, Lord, did it teach me to not deny myself what, at the end of the day, matters most in life: loving freely and strongly, deeply touching another's life and having them touch yours.

The purpose of life is to love. Love strengthens us, it fosters greatness and encourages peace. Still, opening our heart is scary business because there are no guarantees that someone won't break it. It's a spiritual law that what we give is what we get. What we receive from people we love varies. And experiencing occasional pain in our partnerships is unavoidable. But by living with continuous pain in any relationship, we are choosing to suffer, surrendering our power, opting for fear over freedom and love.

Today's women are the first generations of females able to create financial security for ourselves, but many of us with our own financial means stay in relationships that dishonor us because we think staying is best for our children, or we fear flying solo or being criticized by family for the breakup. A stunning number of women stay married to high-profile, wealthy men who abuse them, men who are boldly disrespectful, unfaithful and brutal.

There is often great anxiety in leaving behind what's familiar to us, even though it's hurtful and demeaning. Some of us are stuck in old models and feel we need a man to help us live our dreams, and that a woman is incomplete if she's not somebody's Mrs. We may feel uncertain and halting about how to orchestrate a major transition we know we must make.

When a mother tolerates and trades in disregard and disrespect, her children grow confused and angry; they are being conditioned to become brutal or acceptance junkies. Children will keep our dysfunctional behavior secret, just as my Shana kept mine. But it's too heavy a burden for the little ones to carry, and damage is done. They may develop illnesses and allergies; they may lie, steal, escape into drugs; they may withdraw, slip academically or act out in class.

Men hiding behind abusiveness are also burdened and sad. In a safe place, they may cry a river talking about their childhood pain, usually associated with their father. Renouncing our power to wounded men adds to their injuries. And it's injurious to the whole of society. Wounded, misguided males have been messing up the world for centuries. With today's technology and weaponry they have made the world a very dangerous place.

You can survive anything but self-negation. When a woman tolerates abuse, she gives up her sense of worth, her personhood. No one suffers the loss as she does. What isn't good to you isn't good for you or anyone else. It isn't love.

Life is for loving. If you've settled into a painful relationship, take the risk, take the leap and do something about it. Our partnerships are forever changing. In a sense, all are fluid, unstable—either progressing or degrading. Our love relationships should always be our "project"; they need our attention.

The empowerment of our race is directly tied to our being dedicated to Black love and spiritual growth. Our hunger for bonding, connection, tenderness, and our vulnerability aren't symptomatic of weakness, but of an innate need for love and intimacy. Both women and men must give up the myth of male superiority, which is just another form of bigotry. We have to grow! We have to grow up! We have to cultivate respect and reverence for one another, learn to trust and to turn to one another, and work together, not against one another, for our mighty race to be strengthened and empowered and to catch up.

Talk about your relationship and everything that's ailing you with your partner. Go for counseling if you need help getting started or opening up. Encourage each other to speak freely—and to listen. Get to know the man beneath the makeup. Life takes on new meaning when we stop blaming and start listening. It's the only way to peace in our home and throughout the land. We create a space for healing when we exercise the courage to look at how our own anger and resentment make us withhold love and behave badly.

Difficulty in a relationship doesn't always mean the union should end. Our relationships are our mirrors. But rather than closely observing and monitoring our own behavior, we train our eyes on others, judge them based on our values and unconsciously pick, pick, pick them apart. Stop blaming your partner for your pain and get on with the real business of living, opening your heart fully to love so that you become compassionate and forgiving of yourself and others.

The superficial things that usually attract us to lovers—looks, power, sex—are transitory and won't keep us rushing home to Sweetie for the rest of our life. The you-are-my-everything kind of passion, idealized in adolescence, is an illusion and bound to disappoint. For our relationship to withstand the stress and strain and damage that will have an impact on it over time, there must be mutual respect and admiration between partners.

Never depend on anyone else for your happiness. It's easy to fall into the trap of depending on others for the love, understanding and admiration we all crave, rather than creating them in our relationship with ourself, and bringing the joy in self-fulfillment to our partnerships. When joy is missing in our life, it's missing in our relationships, in our homes and communities.

There's a basic goodness in all of us, "the seed of divinity," says Dudley Thompson, the 91-year-old Jamaican Pan-Africanist and mastermind—a man my husband, Khephra, and I so love. Uncle Dudley agrees that we just get messed up along the way from childhood to adulthood. Even when parents and partners do terrible things, they are just trying in unskillful ways to make their lives work.

Maya Angelou taught me this when I was beating myself down for my own bad behavior: You can only do as well as you know how to do, and when you know how to do better, you do better.

Our relationships are meant to transform us—to make us more compassionate, more loving. Without deep connection, we see only a fraction of others and judge that little piece as all of them. And we think it's our task to change them. We are in relationships to learn to build on the rich soil of love where no one can do anything that is unforgivable. This is not easy. But the walk to forgiveness is our most important walk on Earth. It leads to peace, happiness, deep fulfillment. Focus on being a love finder, not a fault finder.

Not every couple that gets together is meant to stay together. When you're not where God wants you to be, life shakes you up so you'll move to a better place. A fundamental challenge for us all is learning how to move out of unhealthy, unredeemable relationships without slaying one another.

Love him or leave him. When you know it's over, be kind, get your exit plan in gear, sincerely wish him love and happiness, and peacefully get out of Dodge. For our love—and our communities—to thrive, lovers must be friends; we must sincerely like each other. And we must be committed to doing the hard work of living and building together in peace—again and again.

*Your divine right partner is seeking you, may
already be with you. But for love to find its home
in you, your soul must be free and fearless.*

# made for each other

My Uncle Arnold married three times before he swore off love relationships. Movie-star handsome, smart and humorous, he had a steady stream of sisters dropping by his Harlem liquor store trying to catch him. But Uncle was clear. To hear him tell it, partnering was a big headache, and he was much happier living alone.

Then came truth-telling time. In his eighties, just weeks before he made his transition, he admitted that even though he'd had a loving family and friends, there remained a great unfulfilled need in his soul for sharing his life deeply with a mate.

I'll never forget how moved he was by the joy evident between my daughter and "son-in-love." Sitting up in his hospital bed after a visit from Shana and Bernard and witnessing their deep connection and joy, Uncle Arnold spoke volumes about his own life when he whispered this one simple sentence: "That's what it's all about."

Life is a journey to our best self, a journey to God, and relationships are the road we travel. Like us, Uncle Arnold had issues, and they came up in his relationships. We may be masterful at deceiving ourselves, but in our intimate interactions the unresolved feelings and fears we may have buried will surface. Then we can see them and work through them to greater personal and spiritual development.

This is difficult, and most people live and die without doing the deep emotional work necessary to heal and be happy. Many of us sisters feel distrustful of men and swear we'll never let another one get close enough to hurt us again. We may resent the lover who betrayed us a decade ago—the wounded spirit who probably wasn't healthy enough to have a front-row seat in our life in the first place. But our loneliness invited him in. A lover's hurtful behavior in the past is not predictive of the behavior of brothers available to us right now, millions of beautiful Black men longing to love and be loved.

Shunning intimacy helps us maintain the illusion that the problem is with the other person. Our wounds and anxieties can be ignored and left to quietly eat away at our soul and sanity when we're solo and no one questions or challenges us. But the divine purpose of life is self-discovery, and we find opportunities for self-revelation most consistently in intimate relationships—risking, trusting, giving, receiving, sharing soul to soul.

We were created for one another, to come together, to be challenged and tested, and to learn to love and live with our differences. A love relationship is where we practice what we came here to learn: tolerance, patience, commitment and courage, fundamental respect for ourselves and others.

Your divine right partner is seeking you, may already be with you. But for love to find its home in you, your soul must be free and fearless. Choose to love, and choose wisely the person with whom you share your love.

To find your love, you must be willing to be found: Uncle Arnold had this revelation at the end of his life. Don't let that be your story. Try with your whole heart to love wisely and deeply—now!

*We see our relationships as a window on others, but they reflect our own level of emotional and spiritual development. Examine a tense moment between you and another to see how your own actions testify.*

# mirror, mirror

As a girl, I swore I'd avoid the picky criticism that characterized my mother's attitude toward me and so often hurt my feelings. But truth be told, I've become as picky as Babs.

We may see our interactions and relationships as a window on others, but they are more of a mirror reflecting our own level of emotional and spiritual development. Reconsider a disruptive situation you've experienced—an argument, a nasty breakup, a rocky start-up. It's worth examining how your own actions testify.

Recently I had words for a salesperson I felt was racist and would have handled a White customer more courteously. I got annoyed when a woman working in reception at a hotel I was staying at misdirected me when I was pressed for time: I was looking for the business office and she sent me to the gym. And when my husband, Khephra, didn't handle something the way I thought he should—though my beloved is the most reliable person I know—I forgot all about his goodness. I stopped just short of going off, but only just.

Our insecurities and senseless ego demands show up clearly in our interactions with others. And the negative mind-set and faultfinding attitude that drove my bad behavior injured me the most. Anger saps our energy, and it takes time to fade. And each time I go there with Khephra or with my daughter, Shana, I'm chipping away at my most cherished relationships.

It's as though as we travel through life some shadow of ourselves takes pictures of us in all our moments, both of joy and pain. These photographs are stored in our emotional repertoire. When we face turmoil, our "history portraits" are often the faces we show—angry, frustrated faces in all their outdated glory. We're operating with negative feelings brought from another time and place, associated with a whole separate set of issues. We can't create anything good with leftovers from the past.

The most progressive thing we can do right now to nourish our relationships is to begin creating happier lives for ourselves. Heal what hurts you, reduce the stress in your precious life, and step back from living on the edge. We become insensitive and hypercritical when we're overwrought; we get angry at doing the heavy lifting day in, day out without a break. I'm learning what my Babs never did: to leave that dust ball in the corner and go to bed.

When we're sweet to ourselves, we're sweet to others. From an unhappy place, nothing satisfies. From a happy place, common sense prevails. We see clearly that we were born to love, not to judge, and that it's not our job to fix anyone but ourselves. We all have the right to live our life and learn our lessons. When folks don't take the high road, it's because they don't see it yet.

Relationships offer the greatest opportunities for learning and growing at whatever level we are brave enough to choose. Choose deeply intimate relationships, look for your life lessons there, and try living this truth: No matter how others behave, love is the only wise choice for soul and sanity in every situation.

*Looking for love? Honor your covenant with God and you'll want for nothing. Men of dignity will show up. They won't be able to resist you. They'll feel at home with you because you're at home with yourself.*

# the door opens inward

We women love to talk about love. Many of us who are not in relationships can think of nothing we want more. And many of us who have made the connection want those bonds to be closer, deeper and more complete. Women know what makes life work—we know that love is life's fuel, that the love experience makes the life experience better. Love—it's our heart's desire. But often we look outside ourselves to fill the emptiness within.

A woman's search for love is the search for herself, for her own enchantment. But society misdirects girls early on, away from themselves and their feminine power. Over time, we absorb the media's continuous message: "You are not enough; a love relationship is your salvation. Find a man, be sexually intimate and get him to marry you." Society promises that marriage—especially to a man of means—will offer us love and sanction our worth. Believing this exacts a high price from women: It costs us our dignity and power, encouraging fear and neediness—the last thing any secure man wants.

In the 19 years between my two marriages I wore myself out trying to find the right man when I should have been focused on moving out of the basement of my life and into the sunlight. Nothing other than building a bridge of light to our inner beauty, our spirit, will fulfill us.

The rush of romance is delicious but mercurial. It's not the solid stuff lasting love is built on. Finding and appreciating our own rhythm enriches our lives. Then our partners can continue to follow their own rhythm, and it doesn't annoy us. Respect should be our uncompromised requirement for anyone to have a place in our life. Letting go of the expectation that people must fall in line based on our demands frees us and them. It's a gift to the relationship to not be judgmental or insistent.

No person on earth can give you all the love you need—though mutual caring and sharing, combined with sexual intimacy, is desired and oh, so sweet. Your deep yearning for communion originates from your soul and is a yearning for unity with God. It is a longing to experience the greatest part of yourself, the only love you can always count on, the only love that will never leave you.

When a sister is connected to her spiritual core, she has found her glory. She is on fire with desire for living and loving. She's openhearted, full of joy and passion. Her way of living is an expression of reverence for life—for her own and all others—so she's soft and sensitive. She honors above all else her covenant with God, and so she wants for nothing. Men of dignity and faith show up. They can't resist her. They feel at home with her because she's at home with herself. And she's the sisterfriend we women adore. Being with her is nourishing, inspiring and instructive. She's on a journey of self-discovery, trusting in her innate wisdom, and everyone wishes to travel along.

She's the type of partner men long for but have great difficulty finding—a person with whom they can drop their masks and be themselves, a person with the spiritual maturity to be discerning but not judgmental. She knows that a man's greatest gifts are not material or physical; they are on the inside.

If we'll take time every day to focus on our blessings, on what we have, not what we feel is missing in our life, a new joy will fill and satisfy our soul. For our relationships to be healthy and fulfill their divine purpose, the door to our heart must open inward to harmony and cooperation.

*Miss Coretta marveled at what she would have missed had she not looked deeper at the slight and younger Dr. King. In time she found it impossible to resist the man who "made me feel bigger" and changed history.*

# inner vision

"When I first met Martin," Coretta Scott King once shared with me, "he seemed so small, so serious, and he was younger than me. Martin looked like a boy, and I was looking for a man."

Miss Coretta and I marveled at what she might have missed had she looked at Dr. King the way she'd been taught to see, had she not been willing to look deeper, beyond first impressions and outward appearances. In time, she found it impossible to resist the man who would make history. "He made me feel bigger than I am," she said softly, "as if I were already who and what I wanted to be. But that was Martin. He made everyone feel bigger."

In her relationship with young Martin, Coretta Scott King developed insight, discernment, inner vision—the ability to see beauty, possibility and goodness in everyone and everything. We have to make a habit of pausing, observing more carefully without making judgments. This is how we winnow out the wheat from the chaff, see past the outer, beyond the narrow and limited to our larger existence. Insight, not judgment, is what connects us to the highest truth for our learning, and it's at the center of every circumstance.

The loss of a parent, a job, a relationship, our health; environmental neglect; violence in our communities; war in the Middle East—beneath sorrow and chaos is a Divine Order and an invitation to stop struggling against ourselves and one another. Life and our personalities will put obstacles in our way until we come to the way of true seeing: that the face of God is in everything.

Recently there was drama in my family, the kind that distracts my days and brings sleepless nights. Feeling angry and anxious, I forgot what I know: Open your spiritual eye and close the judgmental one. Go deeper, seek the truth, discern the lesson. No matter the trauma, the place of insight and understanding remains the same—the present moment. Get still and centered in it. Turn off the negative thoughts. Shout it out of your mind and heart as I finally did: "No, thank you."

Inner vision and Divine Guidance are ours for the asking, through prayer, meditation or just sitting still. When you ask God for understanding, the light comes shining through. Once I remembered this, within the hour my whole perspective changed. Free from the emotional tangle, I could see the deep truth I was blind to while I sat in judgment: the innocence in what we do when we hurt one another because of our lack of understanding.

Recover the joy if it's missing from your life. Stop thinking about what someone did to you, or didn't do for you, or what you did to yourself. The only way to peace is being at peace with what is. Judgment separates us from the love in us, makes us cranky and hostile. Separation is the source of the friction and suffering everywhere in the world. Harsh judgments and assumptions are so human and cost us so much. Blinded by unexamined impressions, we miss seeing the full spectrum, the amazing grace of the magnificent whole. With spiritual vision, we have discernment and a fuller and more generous view of life. We sense the activity of God in all things, we see the highest and best in others and events.

Love, work that fulfills you, the way to health, wealth and happiness are all right there before you—yours for the taking. All you need to do is pause and ask Spirit to help you see rightly, and as they did for Miss Coretta, the scales will fall from your eyes.

*Joining a man in disrespecting his woman undermines our dignity and integrity. We have lost the key to our own home in settling for a lover who must slip away in the middle of the night.*

# faithful to our sisters

The phone call stunned me. Her voice, soft and sad with its sweet Caribbean lilt, said she was young and in trouble. Vera had told my staff she was a journalism student and wanted to interview me for a class project. But once I was on the phone, she confessed her desperation. Alone in the United States and living in The Bronx, Vera had found a church home, but unwisely began a relationship with a deacon in the congregation who was married. Vera got pregnant, the deacon's wife discovered the affair, and Vera was pushed out of the church in disgrace, but the deacon remained a member in good standing.

I met another sister, a towering bronze beauty, at a weekend retreat who had this to say: "I hurt so bad my eyes ache. Four children, six grandkids and 30 years building our lives together, and in a flash he's gone, living with a girl who's our daughter's age."

And I'll never forget those many years ago when my daughter's frightened twelve-year-old friend wept in my arms: "Mommy and Daddy don't even talk to each other. She cries all the time, and he hardly comes home. Mommy says he has a girlfriend who has a daughter. I bet he'll go away like all my friends' fathers. Then he'll have another daughter, and I won't see him anymore."

We know how hurtful and humiliating it is when a partner betrays us, and that we're not doing God's will when we knowingly cause another person pain. But still, there's so much treachery, betrayal and anger between women competing for men and a stunning amount of "hating" among Black girls. The meanness between young sisters is shocking—it's jealousy turned razor-sharp. Our girls so need loving examples of sisterhood.

How did we get to this state of war between us, when Black women have for so long been shelter to one another? When we could count on no one else, we always knew a sister would have our back. The world still cares little about Black women, so we should be true to each other. Joining a married man in disrespecting another woman by having an affair with him undermines our dignity and integrity. Our wholeness and happiness depend on right choices and right behavior. We have truly lost the key to our own home when we choose a lover who must slip away in the middle of the night or when we settle for filling a gap in a man's broken marriage. We can't build a happy life on someone else's misery. Karma is real: What goes around does, indeed, come around.

The hard truth is, relationships shift and make new rhythms even as we strive to maintain them. All of us are vulnerable. Any of us could find ourselves loving someone who is already committed. Or we could be the one who is in another relationship. If ever we find ourselves in this position, we should turn to truth and to God. Love needs light to bloom, and God answers prayers. If the new love is to flourish, the way will be made clear. We will see the high road to each other, which is always the one that damages others the least.

In all relationships, truth and compassion are the way. It is the road less traveled, but the only one on which our peace and blessings are found.

*Loving a Black man in America can be like welcoming home a war veteran. But who will be allies to our brothers in their personal development if not you and I?*

# a love worth giving

Listen to any group of sisters talking about relationships and you'll hear some complain, "There are no good men out there." But our lives are arranged according to our thoughts, so such statements attract exactly what they call for: no-good men—truth benders and vow breakers. And after having our fill of abuse, we may decide the best we can do is protect ourselves. So we strap our hearts in armor, closing off the very tenderness that draws love near.

My friend Chester Grundy, a vice-president at Kentucky State University, has been married to his wife, Ann, for nearly thirty years. He says, "You sisters have to be patient with us. You're so much further ahead of us brothers in your understanding of life and yourselves."

When men speak from the heart, I listen. Cultural critic and writer Orde Coombs said to me not long before he died, "Brothers don't have the support you women do. We don't have the people or publications or intimate relationships with each other that you have, assuring and affirming and guiding us to live healthy lives."

My husband, Khephra, put it more bluntly: "Some of us simply don't want to grow up."

I'm no apologist for men's hurtful behavior, and I never want to see a woman play the fool. But we can't fully know the burden that Black men carry—the buried hurt, old rage and daddy hunger. The cool indifference, posturing and self-centered player profile are the faces that some brothers front in a society that systematically tries to emasculate them, that has demonized them and built a profit-making prison industry to contain them.

Like us, Black men have had to create their own identity and dignity. Unlike us, they suffer in silence. Loving a Black man in America can be like welcoming home a war veteran. Even brothers at the top of their game are under siege. More than anything, our men need truth and tenderness even when they mess up. The last thing a brother needs is to have us too attacking him.

Who will be allies to Black men in their personal development if not you and I? Who cares more than we do? In all relationships, those with greater awareness have greater responsibility for healing and setting things right. Our communities are in crisis; we have no time to waste.

Choose a man you can love, and work with him. Or commit to understanding more deeply the one you're with. But before any man becomes your lover, make him your friend and, most important, see him as your brother. Don't let little things irritate you. When there's conflict, soften your heart, recognize his innocence—or ignorance—and don't have an attitude. Speak kindly. Be reverent. Practice peace. Be a role model for the behavior that you want him to adopt. As our beloved Dr. Betty Shabazz said she did with Malcolm, find the good and praise it!

*Go on, open your heart wide! Speak the language of love through your tender touch, smiling eyes and affirming words. Be generous with your spirit.*

# fearless love

Fearless, loving communication is the way out of our predicaments—in gender relations, in sustaining family and community, in ending war. And there's no more strategic place to wage fearless love than with our men—because our love is under siege.

Making good love in the middle of war is not easy. But the mighty forces undermining Black love—including our own self-defeating behavior—will wither in the face of open hearts and compassion. Black women's fearless love can unleash great power and restore heart, soul and sanity to our community.

Awaken to the sacred. Our soul work is to see beyond the physical to our deeper humanity. Learn to love goodness, not possessions or power, and the field of exquisite available brothers broadens. Choose honor, kindness, fidelity. Choose one who sees you as his equal, listens when you speak, treats his family well. Take off the mask and work at being your sane, loving self. He'll soon feel safe enough to leave his survival strut at the door. That's success!

Communicate with tenderness and compassion. "I love it when you come to bed early, and we get to laugh and love" gets better results than "All you do is work." Spoken tenderly, honesty is healing, courageous and contagious—and promotes self-respect. Take the lead. Even if your partner communicates poorly, you'll both feel better if you start dropping your verbal defenses and any "meanspeak." Call him sweetly: "Hey, sugar." "Love you, Babycakes." "Hello, handsome; you're the best man on earth."

Consider his feelings. Fight the temptation to point out his flaws. Your opinion is not the truth. Correcting others unnecessarily, frequently or in public robs them of their dignity. As we accept ourselves, we become less judgmental of others, which draws them nearer.

Set personal boundaries. Partners need to know what's not acceptable. If a lover's behavior veers out of bounds, we must protect ourselves physically, financially and emotionally, but it's never our role to punish. If either partner violates a trust but takes responsibility and sincerely wants to repair the damage, recovery is possible. Communication, counseling and new agreements can reestablish trust and even deepen the love. Emotional wounds, like physical ones, take time to heal. Forgiveness occurs in layers.

Be generous with your spirit. Smiling and looking deeply into a person's eyes creates intimacy and connection; it says you're fully present. Smiling eyes communicate approval, trust and admiration and will encourage our men to dream. Brothers need us to believe in them, to be patient with them and to support them as they strive for their goals in their own way, in their own time.

But above all else, we Black women must learn to love ourselves freely, fully and first. Caring for others will always be limited if it doesn't start with self-care and self-respect. Go on, open your heart wide! Speak the language of love through your tender touch, smiling eyes and affirming words. Also listen intently to what your beloved has to say, and make sure that you're hearing it accurately.

Communicating lovingly will keep our partnerships growing strong and see our children through.

*What you give is what you get. Being a sweet and gentle spirit makes you a magnet for love. Send out that invitation, and your divine right partner will find you.*

# invite love in

I hear too many sisters say they're weary of the hurt that love has caused them, and now they'd rather go it alone. But we can't speak of our faith in God, yet despair of finding love—which is God.

Life's larger plan for us includes divine right partnerships. God didn't intend for us sisters to do the heavy lifting alone. But we have to set things right. We have work to do on two fronts: Opening inward, we have to practice loving ourselves well and being the love we want. Expanding outward, we must address the suffocating social and political assaults that are snuffing out Black males and killing our community. The healing begins with us. Believing in love and knowing you are worthy is the first step in birthing a new consciousness within yourself and in every area of society.

Have faith in love; it's all that really matters. We were sent here to learn how to live together in harmony, without inflicting heartbreak or injury. Going solo may seem easier than trying to make love work, but a comfortable, self-centered single life will never challenge you to change and grow or dig as deeply into your soul as a partnership will.

Relationships involve others, but every relationship is with yourself. How you experience someone rests with you. Every choice you make—to be a doormat or to stand in self-respect, to be bitter or compassionate—is yours alone. Relationships bring what we're open to receiving. They are our lifelong workshop on forgiveness, on overcoming selfishness and the need to be right and always in control. Partnering is communion; it's prayer and patient work. Learn to love goodness, honesty and fidelity—not good looks and sweet talk—and the universe of delicious available brothers expands a hundredfold. And what you give is what you get. Being a sweet and gentle spirit makes you a magnet for love. Send out the invitation, and your divine right partner will find you.

There are turning points in our lives, beginnings and endings among friends, lovers and family members too. The very people we love and trust most may hurt us. Who hasn't experienced this? But we survived. We have to learn to look beyond the disguises we all wear and see one another's innocence, the changeless spiritual essence that is the true identity of every person we meet in our lifetime. Pain can be a powerful teacher of compassion. And it can show us how not to be and what not to tolerate ever again.

**Heal the past.** Our happiness doesn't hinge on the actions of others. It flows from deep inside us, from the choices we make. No matter what anyone has done to us, we always have the power to choose a self-loving and self-affirming response. Get professional help if you need it to free yourself of the past and embrace the love waiting for your invitation.

**Keep it juicy.** Take the lead in renewing intimacy. Good sex sweetens a good partnership. I'm trying to work less and rest more so that I'm not so tired and my beloved Khephra can have more of his favorite dessert.

**Be an independent spirit.** Don't sweat what others think about you. Just choose love over conflict, and focus on mastering your emotions and pleasing God. When others hurt you, send love to your own wounds first, then to theirs, rather than trying to make them wrong. Let love rule.

**Bring your joy.** We have lives the generations before ours couldn't have imagined. Remember your blessings, and gratitude will fill your heart. Let laughter loose. Invite love in, and God will pour out blessings in abundance, greater and faster than you can embrace them.

# notes

# notes

# Family Affairs

*Whether our mother is rock-solid or crazy as a loon,*
*whether we're 5 or 55, her words go straight to our heart.*
*They teach us that we are precious, valuable—or not.*

# speak low

I wish that as a young mother I had been more aware of this truth: Everything we say to our children matters. Whether our mother is rock-solid or crazy as a loon, whether we're 5 or 55, her words go straight to our heart. They teach us that we are precious, valuable—or not. Had I known this when I was raising my Shana, I would have measured my words and my tone more carefully.

At times we speak to our children more harshly than we'd ever speak to a colleague or friend—and not just when our children are youngsters. Many daughters greatly love but can't bear spending time with their well-meaning mothers, because each close encounter brings a barrage of humiliating and insensitive remarks: "Meet anybody yet?" "You're getting old, so you'd better stop being so picky and find a man to marry." "You need to fix your hair." "Please lose some weight."

For sons, too, going home can mean suffering hurts from their parents—especially high-achieving ones who often measure their sons by the yardstick of their own accomplishments.

If you're lucky enough still to have your parents, and if they're anything like my beloved Babs was, or even the way I'm still struggling not to be with Shana, everything in your life is up for scrutiny. But as difficult as it is to see, every parent's intention—especially when we pick, pick, pick at every little thing—is always to help our children, not hurt them.

The mother-daughter dyad can be the most complicated and emotionally charged relationship of all, and mothers often lose sight of the boundaries we must respect. We project onto our daughters our own fears and feelings of failure, regrets about opportunities missed and desires and dreams unfulfilled, when what daughters need most is our understanding and affirmation.

Adia majored in industrial engineering and landed a high-paying job after grad school. Over the next decade, her salary and profile rose quickly, but there was no joy. Finally she mustered the courage to follow her passion—painting and printmaking. Gone are the headaches and illnesses brought on by the stress she was under. Adia says she has never been happier, but Moms doesn't understand and is angry, disappointed and loud about it.

For centuries, Black women have been engaged in a painful struggle to maintain sanity and keep our families together and our children safe in a hostile world. In slavery and in freedom, when there was no one to protect us, our mouths have been Black women's greatest weapon and often our only defense. Our voices signify authority, giving us a say-so in our community that few women in the world have yet to command.

Disappointments and threats to our survival over generations have caused legions of us to harden our hearts and bury our sweetness. Many have forgotten the real need we all have—female and male, young and old—for the healing power of a woman's tenderness. Everything in creation needs divine feminine energy— love—to flourish.

Speak low, Ma. Speak tenderly. And you, too, Pa. The most valuable gift we can give our children is the ability to see themselves through the eyes of our love. This will teach them to respect their mind, love their body and trust their heart.

Turn down the volume in your personal and most intimate encounters, and turn it up where it is uniquely justified: in the fight for justice for our children and community.

*Shana had dared to match me word for word. I accused her of being a disrespectful daughter and warned her to mind her mouth. Her truthful response stopped me cold: "Everything I said, I learned at your knee."*

# mind your mouth

That time, for the first time, I responded unemotionally to my mother's insults and harshness. I didn't storm out the door; there were no tears, no attitude. Something in me had shifted. I remember that I was coolheaded and clear, finally able to tell my mother the truth: She'd been hurting my feelings all my life. I was neither the bad girl she had perceived me to be, nor the irresponsible woman of her invention. I wasn't a spendthrift like her mother. I didn't love to run the streets like her sister. And I didn't neglect my child or change men like Liz Taylor. We'd reached an impasse. I made it clear that I wouldn't be calling or visiting until she began treating me with the respect I deserved as a faithful daughter.

Our breach lasted only a week. Babs missed my daily calls. She reached out and apologized as best she could and began taking greater care in how she spoke to me.

Years later my daughter and I were having a heated debate about how she was living and loving. It was clear that she was wrong, and I didn't mince my words in telling her so. It didn't matter that Shana was grown, I was her mother, the only person in her world who would always tell her the truth, blah, blah, blah. She dared to match me word for word. She went too far, and I accused her of being disrespectful and warned her to mind her mouth. Her truthful response stopped me cold: "Everything I said, I learned at your knee."

We pass along, like family heirlooms from generation to generation, our hurts and fears, fossilized into anger and bitterness. We internalize the meanness that's directed toward us and turn it on those most vulnerable in our world. Carelessly, we speak wounding, dismissive words when healing and encouragement are most needed. And we seem to reserve our most severe and belittling verbal attacks for those with whom we feel safest—our children and lovers. It's certainly one of my greatest regrets—the mean-spirited things I've uttered as a mother and a partner when I felt the need to either punish someone or prove myself right.

Simply put, we cannot say everything we think and have peaceful, loving relationships. Apologizing after the heat cools doesn't cancel the hurt that naming and blaming causes.

Two internal voices speak in us, one kindled by fear, telling us we can only be happy if people change to fit our script. This is the voice of attack, the source of pain and abuse in the world. The other, kindled by love, is the voice of God reminding us that happiness doesn't depend on things material or transient, or the mercurial moods and behavior of others.

Living love is simple, but not easy. Our relationships are the mirror in which we practice, practice, practice. Watch your mind and mind your mouth. Make a commitment to love others, but also to love yourself. We're all connected. We don't insult someone and walk away uninjured.

Each time we resist the ego's need to disarm, subdue or punish someone with our tongue, we help that person heal, become better ourselves and strengthen our relationship with God.

*Wrap yourself in kindness. Make this your gift to yourself and your family. No bitterness, no battles, no mean-spirited chitchat. Respond to the right invitations. RSVP to God, to the call for reconnection and communion.*

# holiday presence

A precious and lasting gift I want to give myself and my family this holiday season is freedom from negativity and judgment—loving folks as they are, not fooling myself with the lie that my way is best for them when it's only best for me and I've yet to live up to my own high expectations. During this holiday, sacred to many of us, I want peace in my heart, my family and my home. I want the gift of compassion and sweet communion surrounding me. And I know that to have it I must live it. Loving ourselves and accepting ourselves and others just as we are—these are the challenges and victories of a spiritual life.

We need less—less drama, less stress, less packaging and preoccupation with material things and more love in action. Peace on Earth, joy to the world, Happy New Year, Merry Christmas, Happy Kwanzaa: These are the sentiments we will express this season. But our loneliness, nameless fears and anxieties scream for more than empty words and forced cheer.

Before accepting the endless invitations to empty our wallets, before the commercial hysteria peaks to a fever pitch, turn toward what is true: that place in your heart that knows the indwelling Christ. Take a few moments early each morning to think about your one and only life, your sacred self, to speak and listen to it. It takes a lot of energy to dull the soul and not hear its voice. Fortunately, it's a voice that will not be ignored. It will knock on the door as fear, depression, debt or illness until we awaken to our purpose and commit to fulfilling it.

The Christ Spirit in you is waiting to be reborn as you. You are the second coming you've been waiting for, and wherever two or more of us are gathered together in that universal love and compassion, whenever the Christ Spirit is allowed to live in us, healing and helping us, it will shine so radiantly that others will seek and see it in themselves. This should be our sacrament, our communion, our offering to God this holiday season. No matter what our religion, as we prepare for a new year, let's reach for that spirit of love within us, and let us see beyond people's pain and personalities to the Christ in them as well. Being aware that we are the presence of God on earth helps turn negativity into mist, and panic into patience and peace. What greater gift could we give? What more could we ask?

This season I'm wrapping myself in kindness. This is my gift to myself, to my family and our community. I'm unwrapping the deeply divine in our children—so many are suffering and crying out for our love and support. This holiday season I'm not jumping into the fray, but examining whether people and events support my divine purpose or detract from it. No bitterness, no battles, no clutter, no mean-spirited chitchat. I'm going to respond to the right invitations. I'm going to RSVP to God, to the call for reconnection and communion, accepting the invitation that's always there to expand our happiness and comfort, and to bring healing to ourselves and others. I'm going to host a party with Divine Love as my honored guest.

We can take the advice of Brother Lawrence, the Carmelite who centuries ago said the most important discovery in his entire life was that we can transform a little rough cabin into a palace just by flooding it with the light of God. Let us make this our offering.

*I'm a lovebug, but my parents, Babs and Lawrence, never seemed to touch or talk to each other much. Likewise, touching and tenderness were absent in any communication between them and me.*

# it's love!

Over a childhood of summers—all before I was ten—I experienced a feeling of confidence and comfort that I've been working to reclaim all my adult life.

Come summer, my grandmother Rhoda Weekes would rescue my brother, Larry, and me from our cramped Harlem apartment and take us to her rambling 13-room home in Englewood, New Jersey.

Crossing the Hudson River in Mother's big black Buick, I entered a new world—one where I felt cherished. Mother would give me lots of hugs and kisses. She'd do magical things with my thin, woolly hair and "grease" my skinny brown legs till they'd glow.

There was freedom and adventure too. I'd catch fireflies, dance in the rain, jump the ocean waves at the shore. I could ride my bike all day and believed that if I dared lift my wings I could rise and soar like an eagle. When I was with Mother, I was the sky and the surf. I felt safe and connected to everyone and everything around me.

At summer's end I'd go back to Harlem, which was being overrun by heroin, robbing us children of our freedom, narrowing our world. I was back in my bustling neighborhood where I always felt sad and alone. I'm a lovebug, but my parents, Babs and Lawrence, never seemed to touch or talk to each other much. Likewise, touching and tenderness were absent in any communication between them and me. And in school, the Irish nuns who taught me didn't hide their disdain for the Black children in their charge.

We do come to adulthood with issues. Their role is to teach us to pay attention to our thoughts and feelings. Our hurts and uncomfortable emotions had a reason for being. Let them flow through us without judging them good or bad or holding on to them. Otherwise they hold us hostage.

The heartache I lived with most of my childhood and believed was my greatest misfortune is the very thing pushing me forward along the path of wisdom. Feeling unloved and "unlovely" makes me consciously try to be loving and to acknowledge the beauty of our little Black girls. When I became a mother it encouraged me to create a loving household for my beloved Shana.

God is loving and wise. As a girl, over a decade of summers, I got a sense of how it felt to be loved and radiantly alive. As a woman, my work is to live in that state of grace, to more and more be that perfect love—to live it and give it to myself and bring it wherever I go or wherever I feel it is lacking.

It's love! Loving is the work we are called to do, our responsibility and the joy of life.

Wherever your suffering lies—in your relationships, with health, career or financial challenges—it didn't come your way to haunt you or daunt you, but to soften your heart and teach you to love more deeply and fully. Consciously act to counterbalance pain of any kind with an abundance of love.

We can dissolve our suffering. Everything we need for our healing—a counselor, a nutritionist, a gym, a new career, a new attitude or perspective—awaits our call. Make the move.

# notes

# Forgiveness

*Don't take anyone's bad behavior personally. It's about them, not you. In the life God has in mind for us, love is our only weapon, the assured defense against any offense.*

# choose love as your weapon

"Don't fight!" We all grew up hearing it. Yet throughout our lives, conflict is ever near: Violence is entertainment—on TV, in movies and video games. It pervades our history lessons, the nightly news, even cartoons created for children. Trouble is, we learn how to be by watching and imitating. And what we learn is to strike back when someone hurts us. Retaliation! Put 'em up! Get ready for the big payback!

I have lived in that painful place. When a long-ago lover struck me, I didn't just let go of the relationship, I found a way to pay him back. But the thrill of vengeance didn't restore my sense of self-worth. In fact, life slapped me around. Being vindictive closed me off to all the joys around me, made me cynical, eventually ill. Even when we feel justified, we can never strike out at another soul without wounding ourselves. At the fifth dimension, that spiritual level where healing takes place, we are called to demonstrate love and mercy, even toward those who would hurt us. In the life God has in mind for us, love is our only weapon, the assured defense against any offense.

Don't take anyone's bad behavior personally. It's never about you. We're all growing up together. When someone tries to slay you, choose love as your weapon, keep your heart open, even if you must back away and let go of the relationship. Seek the deeper truth, the lesson Spirit seeds in each of our experiences. Only an open heart understands that everyone who enters our life is a guest bearing a gift. Sometimes we must seek out the gift, as my beloved friend Ellin LaVar did.

Ellin's been braiding my hair since she was 16 and is like a daughter to me. In the years I've known her, she's grown to be a queen in the hair-care industry and has many celebrity clients. Recently one of the divas, because of some perceived offense, went off on Ellin in the salon, shouting, screaming and swearing. Ellin, a serious, take-no-mess sister, was mortified and humiliated. But she resisted joining in a cutting contest and quietly kept weaving the sister's hair.

Looking back, Ellin says that day was a turning point for her because she managed to hold on through hurt, anger and betrayal to get to the lesson. But first she had to win a war within herself: She had to subdue her own ego and choose love. In a flash, she had seen shades of herself in the sister's outburst and realized that she, too, at times has had trouble expressing her feelings without anger. This time she quietly checked herself and decided not to head down the same path. In making that choice, she grasped what few people do: There can be no victory when we victimize another.

Today Ellin's growth is bringing her bountiful blessings: Her hair-care products, Textures, are winning at retail, and her reality show, *Hair Trauma*, was picked up for another season. It's always like that when we choose to be a spiritual warrior who wields but one weapon: love. Love heals everything; nothing good is ever lost. Choosing love over ego and indignation takes consistent work. It also takes the will to move to a higher emotional and spiritual plane where God can use you to bring needed healing to our troubled world. It's no more complicated than putting our ego on pause and asking of every painful encounter: How can I meet this with enough understanding and love to see the gift being offered to me? Be grace. Wield love as your only weapon, and you place yourself on the path to self-mastery, bountiful blessings and the perfect peace we are all longing for.

*We all make mistakes. We all mess up. And we'll always*
*feel frustrated expecting in us humans what is found only in*
*the Divine. Only God is perfect in every way, all the time.*

# seventy times seven

Who doesn't have a painful story to tell about rejection or abandonment, about emotional or physical abuse? Who hasn't been hurt by a parent, a lover, or even a stranger? And who hasn't hurt another or injured themselves? The anguish we harbor from unhealed wounds is deep. We dull and deny the aches by drinking and drugging, overworking, overspending, even adopting a veneer of sweetness or subservience. Forgiveness is the way to healing our addictions and fears, but it is not possible without the honest revelation of our feelings.

We all need a safe place where we can be emotionally vulnerable and can examine and understand the traumatic experiences in our life. And what a blessing it is to have access to so many healing techniques and therapies: prayer, meditation, daily respites of inward listening, psychoanalysis, rebirthing, dance and music therapy, journal writing, beating the pillow, finding a private place to scream if you must.

A few years ago I decided to work with a therapist to unearth the hurt I buried as a little girl whose feelings weren't understood or respected. I didn't intend to carry any mountains on my shoulders into the new year.

It takes courage to shine a light into the dark corners of our life, the very last places we want to look. But pain informs; that's its purpose. Analyzing our emotional pain won't crush us, as the ego fears, but will open us to a deeper and wiser understanding of our wounds, their causes and effects.

Eric Harris and Dylan Klebold, the White teenagers at Columbine High School in Colorado who murdered their schoolmates and a teacher, weren't the monsters the media portrayed them to be. The monster is the culture of violence that makes heroes of hit men. Like the rap music that celebrates gangster life and disrespect of women, which has captivated so many young Black males, death metal music, equally lethal, has influenced White youths like Eric and Dylan. Behind the bands' incessant screaming guitars are lyrics about devil worship, blood and bondage; about killing people, eating babies and suicide. The groups' names are telling: Satan Underground, Morbid Angel, Cannibal Corps. Eric and Dylan, two deeply disturbed children, were sad and lonely boys who were taught—as all our boys are—to hide their fears and sorrows, to put on their game face, to "man up!"

Everywhere the nightly news testifies about how not attending to our wounds makes us psychologically fragile, how it can push folks over the edge. We all need at least one someone whom we can trust with our truth. We need a safe place to talk about our anger, sadness and wounds, where we can discern and heal the overwhelming emotions that arise in us. Otherwise we construct a wall around our heart, blocking love and wisdom. This makes us ill. Medical research is now confirming what many ancient spiritual practices have long taught: Resentment and the unwillingness to forgive are major sources of disease.

Anger and the desire for retaliation can consume us. The very people we are angry at we make paramount in our lives, linking them to us in a highly charged emotional connection. We yoke them to us. Only forgiveness can break the unhealthy bond. Releasing the pain and replacing it with love for God is a choice we can make. It takes courage and commitment.

When we don't take responsibility for our behavior and feelings, we give up our power. People cause us pain when they are in pain, struggling and not attending to their spiritual growth. Feeling anger toward those who've hurt us puts our power in their unsteady hands. And it not only blinds us to their essence, the abiding love and kindness that is their true nature; it also blinds us to our own.

Choosing to forgive those who've hurt you doesn't affect them, but it does affect you deeply. It liberates you, releasing you from the prison of anger, hurt and guilt. It softens your heart and opens the door to love and health, abundance and peace.

The way to forgive others is to forgive yourself for your own missteps, large and small, and the hurt you have caused others. We all make mistakes and will be frustrated as long as we expect in us humans what is found only in the Divine. Only God is perfect in every way, all the time. Ask God to help you move beyond judging to understanding. The Gospel teaches: As you forgive, so are you forgiven.

Though many people disappointed Jesus, he constantly taught forgiveness. If Jesus could forgive his apostles who betrayed him, if he could ask God to forgive his murderers, what is so wounding that we can't forgive? Forgive all who hurt you. Forgive yourself for hurting yourself. Not once, not twice, but, as our beloved brother Jesus taught us, seventy times seven—again and again, forevermore.

*Forgiveness is a faith issue. And faith doesn't come immediately or easily. We must work at it. When we put our trust in love, we are released from the past that causes sadness and suffering.*

# faith and forgiveness

It wasn't that my mother, Babs, didn't love her mother, but that the bold choices my grandmother made as a young woman hurt and shamed Mommy; they broke her heart.

After divorcing my grandfather, Arnold Weekes, in Trinidad, Rhoda emigrated to the United States, leaving her six children in her own mother's care. My grandmother had taken a lover back home, the husband of her good friend, and she brought him to the States first, before sending for her mother and the children. Once her lover was with her in New York, Mother and Cecil Innis lived together and built businesses together over the years. Mr. Innis eventually sent for his wife and children, who were friends with the Weekes children.

The three households were all in Harlem—Mother and Mr. Innis living together; Mommy and her siblings with their grandmother, Susan; and Mrs. Innis living with the Innis children.

What a mess!

All were in the same community—fractured, split apart, nursing bitterness. Mommy never let go of the fury and shame she felt, carrying the burden of her anger from childhood to her grave.

In the arc of our lives, people fail us, even family and friends. So what do we do when our heart hurts or our trust has been shattered? My grandmother came to this country in 1916. Mommy died in 1991. That's 75 years of rage that Babs was host to. Even if our anger is justified, we are the ones who suffer most from harboring it. Anger creates bitterness, which has great power. It can destroy the host.

We continuously injure ourselves by keeping old wounds open. This is why forgiveness is so important. We don't hear the voice of the Divine when rage and resentment are screaming inside us. The unwillingness to forgive disconnects us from God, sets us at odds with what is holy. This is why all the great spiritual traditions teach us to practice forgiveness. "Father, forgive them for they know not what they do" were Jesus' most memorable words.

The way of the world is to carry rage. The news, national and international, is all about strife and struggle, the fight to the finish. An eye for an eye leaves everyone blind. Continuing friction leaves everyone raw. It's the fallible way, not God's way.

Strife anywhere in your life is a call from God to love more. Friction anyplace in your life is God speaking loudly to you—telling you plainly, "Seek harmony, seek peace, seek Me." The day you consciously answer the call, everything in your life gets better, grows richer. You see the spiritual poverty of those who wounded you. Your own misery resolves when you see the pain they are in. You understand that people who are hurting will hurt others, and the deeper their pain, the greater their need is for love and compassion.

The love we give is always received on the spiritual level. Our ego tells us the love has to be acknowledged our way. Forgiving never means tolerating bad behavior. It's a wise choice, a willingness to let go of the past and take a spiritual leap forward, forgiving others as God forgives you.

Forgiveness is a faith issue. And faith doesn't come immediately or easily. You have to work at it. Forgiving is an opportunity to do the work, to put our trust in love and be released from a past that is causing us sadness and suffering.

Let the sun set on yesterday. Start life anew today. If you have trouble forgiving, emulate Jesus. Ask God to do the forgiving, and you do the work of letting go.

# notes

bundance

*Life doesn't compensate you based on the activity of work alone, but also on the activity of your consciousness. Envision, believe, plan, take action, give back. These create the natural abundance God wants for you.*

# living abundantly

Every time I meet a Black woman living fully and freely in retirement, I'm inspired. And I tune my ear. I learn lots by listening to a sister like Alneta Chambers, my former coworker's mother, who had sold her Long Island home to her daughter and son-in-law so she could retire to Atlanta along with some friends. "I'm financially secure in my golden years because I tried to make smart career and money moves when I was a young single mother raising Darlene and working for the U.S. Postal Service, where I was employed for 29 years," she says.

When Darlene was 12, Alneta, a mail clerk, took a few night classes. She trained to be a travel agent, took courses in real estate and business management, and one in accounting, which helped her qualify for a higher-paying position in the postal service's financial department. "The more I earned, the more I saved," Alneta says. "I contributed a percentage of my pay to what we then called the Thrift Savings Plan and also to my government pension fund." She didn't touch the money that was building up except for her and Darlene's education.

Like so many of us, Alneta had a couple of gigs. She worked as a travel agent, was paid by the state for keeping an elderly person in her home, and, when Darlene went off to college, became a foster mother for two years. "I made it a habit to invest between $7,000 and $8,000 each year in my mutual funds and, over a ten-year period, $100 a month in U.S. Savings Bonds," she remembers proudly.

I first met Alneta Chambers having fun with her womenfriends in New Orleans. They'd traveled there to attend our "Party With a Purpose," The Essence Music Festival, over the Fourth of July weekend. A week later she was visiting us at *Essence* headquarters in New York City and showing off her new grandbaby. In August she went on a Caribbean cruise with her church, in September to the National Baptist Convention in Kansas City. At the time Alneta was living in a large two-bedroom apartment in Atlanta and preparing to purchase outside the metro area. "But whatever I settle on," said the youthful, joyful grandmother, "must have a pool. While I was working and raising Darlene, I had to make so many sacrifices. Now I want and can afford the best!"

The financially sound life Alneta Chambers is living is the natural outcome of working with the creative ideas Spirit sends us all to fulfill ourselves and do good for others. Prosperity is our birthright. But too often, though God wants to shower us with abundance, we have small expectations.

If you're struggling financially, living beyond your means or not investing in your future, your anxiety is a prompting from God to begin rethinking and redirecting your life. You have to outsmart credit card companies. They want to string out your debt forever, which is why monthly minimum payments are low—so you are paying them interest for decades while your debt continues to mount.

Start with your highest-interest-rate credit card and pay much more than the required minimum. Never pay less. And stop using credit cards. When you've wiped out that debt, add the amount you paid on that card to the monthly payment of the next-highest-rate card and repeat this until you're totally free of credit-card debt.

You know how you would like to be living this time next year. You have at least an idea of where you'd like to be five, ten or twenty years from now. Remember this before spending, and begin laying the groundwork to realize your dream. Within you lie the talent and ingenuity to create everything you need throughout all the transitions in your lifetime. Turn your passions into profit or, like Alneta Chambers, get a couple of gigs on the side.

Forgive yourself for unwise spending, and stop any moaning about how you may have messed up your money. Have no regrets. No beating yourself up because an investment failed, or you bought a new car that's worthless today, instead of buying a house. Those thoughts just block the doors to abundance and prevent you from seeing the many wise choices you also made. Put your mind to creative ways of increasing your net worth instead of worrying. Create in your mind the prosperous life you want and let go of the stories that don't support financial success. And keep giving wisely with an open heart and no strings attached. Give away furniture, appliances, clothing, books that are no longer useful to you. Bless others, and greater blessings will come to you. The more freely you give, the more abundance you will receive.

Give yourself to life, give the best of yourself to serving others—just as Alneta Chambers did. Contribute lovingly by bringing the highest level of integrity to all that you do—with your colleagues, clients, family, friends and folks you may never see again. Service will always return to you tenfold as prosperity.

Life doesn't compensate you based on the activity of work alone, but also on the activity of consciousness. Envision, believe, plan, take action, give back. All these together will create the natural state of abundance that God so wants you to enjoy.

*Material riches are merely the realization of love and life's abundance. They are the physical evidence of self-love, honoring the Presence within, and your value and worth.*

# from center to circumference

We choose circuitous and complicated routes to prosperity. We move across the country, change our jobs and professions, our image and our partner but bring along the same impoverished spirit and then wonder why we're still poor and in pain. There are those who win millions in the lottery and slip back into poverty, and those who gain the world and lose their soul.

Our wealth isn't tied to the economy or to good luck or to the largesse of others. Our wealth is in our consciousness; it is Spirit-based. Every soul has come to earth to learn this lesson. At some time in our lives we will have to surrender our need for money to God because everything in the outer world has failed us. This coming to faith gives us the opportunity to demonstrate for ourselves and others the source of money and any success.

Holding the highest thoughts about giving and receiving is the source of all prosperity. Life flows smoothly when you are loving yourself, giving value to others and working to make life better for those in need; the abundance in the universe supports your dance and becomes your partner. Everything you need to help God create a better world is at your fingertips. Focus on changing life for the better and your intuition opens, you make the best possible choices, and high-level guides direct your path and ensure your purpose.

To not have a life of abundance takes effort; it takes resisting the gifts and talents God has given us; it takes believing that your life and creative ideas are not important; it takes rejecting the call to leadership and what your soul beckons you to do.

You don't have to commit to a job you don't like or toil until you're exhausted to earn a good living. For centuries, the generations before ours worked for nothing and little more than nothing. The Western world owes the Black world a great debt. Our free labor made European countries rich and the United States the wealthiest nation on earth. Without question, a great debt is owed to us. Stand strong for reparations, but don't wait on a check. The arc of the moral universe is long but it bends toward justice, as Dr. Martin Luther King said. This is our time to rise. The wind is at our back. We only need to trust and love ourselves and one another more, to work together better.

Give yourself permission to be and do what you want. Open your heart to what you love doing and become the very best at it you can possibly be. Make it your vocation, your contribution to the world. Through the day every day say thank you to God—even for the small things you take for granted like running water, the food on your table, your eyes, ears and feet that work. We are wealthy in ways we do not notice. Be grateful for all you have and your wonderful life. Be grateful to God, the ancestors who suffered greatly, and those who raised you. Be grateful also to yourself for surviving and staying the course.

Sanaya Roman and Duane Packer, two wise souls who channel their wisdom, have this to say about creating prosperity in our lives:

> Every time you experience something you like, you can create even more of it in your life by using a process called "amplifying." For instance, say you have just experienced or received something you want more of. Stop for a moment and let the joy of having it grow stronger. Feel the satisfaction in your body, emotions, and mind. Then get quiet and imagine yourself amplifying that energy. Imagine those feelings are growing like a spiral of energy, starting

*in your heart and becoming the size of your body or even larger. By doing this you are making yourself magnetic to even more good things. Pretending that you are increasing your feelings of satisfaction and happiness, plus intending to have more good things appear in your life, is all that is required.*

Yes! Notice what you have and it expands. "And so it is," is what my beloved friend Reverend Andriette Earl, of East Bay Church of Religious Science in Oakland, says after each prayer, each affirmation, to seal all the good she wants made manifest in our lives.

Pay your bills on time and feel joy when you are writing checks and meeting your financial obligations. Otherwise you're calling lack into your life, hosting scarcity and expanding it. Look around you and you'll see the evidence of your faith, what you believe in.

Spiritual growth is the path; material riches are merely the realization of love, of life's abundance. They are the physical evidence of self-love, honoring the Presence within and your value and worth. When we love and value ourselves, we don't deny ourselves the things we need, and we open our hands for giving and receiving.

Seek the kingdom first! That's all God asks of us. Start from within, stay conscious of the Presence, focus on knowing and loving yourself, work from the center to the circumference, and everything you want and need will come to you. Your outer world is caused by your consciousness: As within, so without. We live and move and have our being in a universe of wonder, abundance, beauty and balance. All that God has created is flowing freely all around us and is ours to experience and share. Everything in the universe is for us. God is the giver of life; we are the receivers.

In silence, sit or lie down and place both hands over your heart. Close your eyes; breathe deeply, rhythmically. Divine Intelligence is always at work, leading us toward our purpose, trying to show us how to claim prosperity—wealth, health and joy. Stay focused on breathing deeply and steadily; remember that your breath is the Holy Spirit residing in you. Ask Spirit to release any guilt you may have about money and help you see abundance as your birthright. Ask your soul what it is longing for. Ask your heart what it must give to life and receive to feel fulfilled. Don't hurry the answers. They will come when you're ready to receive them, sometimes in a flash, sometimes unfolding over time. Listen to your inner guide. Trust and surrender to the higher power within you.

Impoverished thoughts and negative attitudes have replicated themselves as the poverty and misery all around us. But even this is part of the master plan, life's way of coaxing us toward enlightenment, repeatedly asking us to choose the high road and to answer these critical questions: Will you come home to yourself? Will you take inventory, let go of the human and put your faith in the divine? Will you focus on the life within you before the world around you?

Having the finer things in life definitely has its place in my world. But what I know now that I didn't know in my twenties, thirties and forties is that everything we have we can lose. But everything we are keeps growing richer, brighter, better over time. And nothing and no one can take that away.

Nourish your inner life and develop an intimate and trusting relationship with God. This is the basis of everything Jesus came to teach us and the core tenet of the world's great religions. We put too little faith in this wisdom because the principle seems so simple. Yes, it is simple—and true. Seek first the kingdom of God within you and everything you need shall be given unto you.

*Don't sweat where you are right now; it's your blessed entry point.*
*Step toward your greatness, your highest aspirations, step into your name.*
*By the power of your trust and faith, the way will open wide.*

# lead the change

It's a great blessing to do work that is meaningful, enjoyable and so in tune with your spirit that you arise excited to greet the day. Work is love. It's one of the ways in which we contribute to life and grow in grace and greatness. But look at the weary faces in your family, your workplace and perhaps in the mirror. We spend most of our waking hours earning a living, and many of us feel miserable doing it. We stay in jobs that aren't satisfying, complaining that we are undervalued, overworked and underpaid, all because we fear change.

Life is change. Welcome it! Every unhappy day that passes without your taking steps toward reinventing your life roots you more deeply in misery. It doesn't help that so many of us, immersed in a culture of celebrity, see fame and fortune as the goal. We even celebrate stars who behave badly, who are the poorest role models for our children. Instead, let's lift up those who are leading change, fighting against hunger, HIV/AIDS, disrespect of Black womanhood, violence in our world. At the end of the day, what we've earned, the homes we've acquired, are no comfort. The true source of our peace is knowing that we are exercising our power and resources to help those less fortunate, that we are using what we have at hand to be a leader for change.

Start at home. Take the leadership role in your life and career. This is where your strategic advantage lies—in following your heart and preparing for what is nourishing to your spirit. Don't sweat where you are right now; it's your blessed entry point. Fashion a plan to help you boldly leap forward in this rapidly changing global economy, rather than reacting after the fact to events forced upon you by shrinking Social Security, health and pension benefits.

Plan now! No matter how much you believe your organization values you today, your tomorrows are vulnerable. Pressed to increase profits every year and forevermore, the also-vulnerable, ever-changing guard at the top is forced to make shortsighted changes that will stunt the lives of unprepared workers. And yet your tomorrows are also full of promise and opportunity: Enter into a covenant with yourself to create new streams of income, including ventures you will profit from in retirement and pass along to the younger generation. Ask yourself, *Where do I want to go next?* Identify what's not working and visualize the life you want to be living by summer, at year's end, five years from now. Hold steady your vision, and no matter what, don't give up.

Assemble your dream team, your supporters, your board of directors, your confidants, those who can help you build the life of your intentions: the financial mind who'll help you up your money and put the right digits in the right columns, the mentor who's a star in the field you want to succeed in, young people who bring passion and energy, retirees who can help you tackle the tasks, and your counselor or spiritual guide—seek and welcome from them strategies and advice that are right with your soul.

Step toward your greatness. As an honor to God, step into your name. Join the vanguard of visionaries who are redefining success and the purpose of work from solely making money to making a better society. Pursue your highest aspirations, and by the power of your trust and faith, the walls will tumble and the way will open wide. The new life you want is waiting for you.

*Keep your eyes open as you travel the paths in your own community. Notice what needs to be addressed and start making or expanding your entrepreneurial plans.*

# breaking ground

Four years ago Naomi Sabel was a young college student on her way to class when she spotted a For Sale sign on a lot in a desolate area fifty miles outside of Cleveland. Each day she passed the property and thought somebody ought to do something with it. "There didn't seem to be a whole lot of candidates," she said. "Not understanding the obstacles, I didn't see what others had seen: the 500 reasons why developing it would be difficult. I saw opportunity."

Naomi also had a dream that wouldn't quit. She enlisted two fellow students, who became her business partners. None of them had any experience in real estate development. With private and public funding, their company, Sustainable Community Associates, is developing a $15 million project, the first major commercial development in historic downtown Oberlin, Ohio, since 1958. The complex, a mix of market-rate condos, affordable rental units and retail space for local proprietors, will also have 10,000 square feet of open-air space for community concerts and markets.

The citizen sector, a new breed of visionary leaders, is emerging in communities throughout the world. They are social entrepreneurs, creating profit-making enterprises that seek to lessen the social blight that governments are ignoring. They are the wave of the future, people who know that we can change the world. Black women and men should be in the vanguard.

Keep your eyes open as you travel the paths in your own community. Notice what needs to be addressed and start making or expanding your entrepreneurial plans. Government grants, tax subsidies and resources from foundations are available to help restore lives and communities. This is how Rising Tide Capital, a Jersey City enterprise cofounded by Alfa Demmellash, an Ethiopian-born entrepreneur, and Alex Forrester, her Harvard classmate, continues to grow and serve. "Fighting Poverty Through Entrepreneurship" is the young founders' motto. By offering training at their Community Business Academy and connecting graduates to capital and business coaches, they are assisting underserved people, including the disabled and those coming out of prison, in opening businesses. As these young visionaries know, we can do good and do well.

If you are a business owner or just giving birth to the entrepreneurial spirit, no matter what the enterprise, you can add a not-for-profit component that will make the world a better place, like providing training to young people who've gotten off track or quality day care for struggling families.

Monumental advances in technology have "flattened" the world and connected people everywhere, giving us Black folks huge opportunities to scale up. Information that was once inaccessible or expensive is now at our fingertips and free. Do your due diligence. Surround yourself with the pros you need to put a polished business plan in place. Join the local chamber of commerce for immediate information, exposure and connections. Shoo all the negaholics out of your life. There is more than enough wealth in the economy to finance your effort. Fill your mind and heart with visions of the success of your enterprise and then figure out how to give back.

With faith, focus and a flexible plan, we can secure our financial future, build much-needed multigenerational wealth, and serve our community. God is lavish, unfailing abundance. Remember the Word: Beloved, I wish above all things that thou prosper.

*The Lord is my shepherd.... Remembering and believing just one spiritual truth overrides fear and a thousand negative thoughts.*

# imagination: the dream weaver

Today I have a zest for living, but there was a time when I felt stuck—when it seemed that nothing in my life was working. Money would slip through my fingers. I never had enough. Now I can see that my own faulty thinking had come between me and my hopes and dreams. Although I didn't tell anyone, inwardly I would tear myself down, would compare myself unfavorably with the many smart, skilled and amazing people in my world. And my impoverished thoughts and habits—dream killers—did their destructive work: They created circumstances and experiences that mirrored them.

We underestimate the power of the master controller, our imagination. This is how the mind's creative intelligence works: What is impressed on our subconscious is magnified, multiplied and made real in the world. What you give your energy to, you get more of. Everything in the universe is a form of energy. The material and nonmaterial are more similar than the naked eye can see. Things that appear to us as solid—clothing, walls, furniture, automobiles—appear as molecules in motion under a high-powered microscope. Energy is materialized through thought. This is how we form our personal world—with our imagination.

We create our own reality and can learn to use this amazing power to our great benefit. Limiting thoughts create a limited life. When fearful thoughts or self-criticism come, slay them by contemplating and embodying the truth: My God shall supply all my needs....I am made in the image and likeness of the Creator. . . . The Lord is my shepherd, I shall not want. Remembering and repeating just one spiritual truth overrides a thousand negative thoughts.

If we're not watchful, though, negativity seeps into our daily life and consumes us. Our hopes and dreams dim; we adjust and hardly notice. But our heart notices. The heart is where God speaks to us. When we follow our heart and our passion, we find joy and abundance. With inner harmony, outer harmony unfolds. As I dedicate more time and effort to our underserved children—which I've learned is my divine assignment—my life grows richer.

To get on with what God created us to do, we have to cancel our puny thoughts about ourselves and life the moment they occur and replace them with true, loving and affirming beliefs. They help us grow and shape our life according to the divine reality, which has no limits. Our imagination is a portal to every possible world. We can choose any one of them.

Do what you love and prosperity will follow. Money is just part of it. The greater part is the clarity you gain about why you are here, and the confidence you feel in where you are headed. Your life grows greatly in depth, breadth and meaning.

Do you. Maybe you're bored with your work. Discontent is divine intervention, God's way of encouraging you to reexamine your life and use your unique gifts. As you do more of what you are called to do, you create abundance in the highest measure: peace, prosperity, joy. You become more passionate about the things that matter most to you.

Do what you love. Write, paint, plant, design clothing or Web sites, plan events. Do it for you, and do it in service to God. As you give, so you will receive. Do what you love and you will see ways in which you can turn your passion into a business that spreads happiness.

Transitions aren't always seamless, and success may not happen overnight. Look honestly at your skills and do the work to close any gap between them and your dreams. I did—and I'm still doing it. So I could be a better editor and leader, I went to college for the first time when I was in my mid-thirties and the head of the magazine. Now it's a more direct type of service to the community that I'm passionate about, working with one of the most dedicated leaders in the nation, my friend and president emeritus of the National 100 Black Men of America Inc. Tommy Dortch, on building the National Cares Mentoring Movement to secure our most vulnerable youngsters; next is community development. I've learned that nothing new and great is created from the imagined safety of our comfort zone.

Master your mind. Dedicate yourself to teaching your mind to hold positive images and thoughts. Whatever it is you want to do or achieve, see yourself doing and achieving it. As you make the stretch, forces seen and unseen will support and advance you. The person you are destined to become is God's great idea.

*Take your life back. Don't be held hostage by 24/7 connectivity or working like mules. Break away from the pack. Less is more, and slower is faster. Your life awaits your attention and dedication.*

# make it easy on yourself

We release our struggles when we begin to see life as a teacher and a good friend, not a foe. Otherwise we spend our time feeling afraid—like kids who frolic under a bright noon sky, then close their eyes tight and act frightened in the dark. Open your eyes. See the brilliant light all around you. What brings you joy and fulfillment is God's wish for you. Making these critical moves will help God help you live fully in the light.

Come out of hiding. Find a safe place to express your emotions freely. Hiding is so stressful and creates shame, anger and illness. A trusted friend or a therapist can help us speak our deepest secrets and fears. Giving voice to them melts blockages, helps us heal.

I used to be so ashamed of the early sexual activity I had engaged in as a girl, and I carried a knot of shame in my stomach from the time I was ten. I didn't understand that I wasn't a bad girl, only a child seeking love. The shame was uprooted when I answered the call to speak to women in recovery from drug addiction—they became my path to freedom. Facing women who thought I would never understand the sexual compromises they had made to feed their habit, I found myself sharing my secret shame. In that moment, the burden I had carried for so long was lifted. I felt free! What causes us pain has to be honored, heard and validated so that we can release it and heal. If someone rejects you based on what you've lived through, it's a gift, life telling you to cut that tie.

Be determined. Don't let anyone put a damper on your dreams. Work toward a goal that's for the highest good, and your spirit will prepare you to achieve it. Remember that for a full year and 16 days, 42,000 Black people in Montgomery, Alabama, boycotted public transportation and walked to wherever they had to go, crippling a bus system and toppling a legal system that denied our humanity. Fill your heart with faith, knowing that God doesn't give you a mission without also giving you the power to bring it to fruition. Keep stepping, no matter what.

Make wise investments. Get the best financial adviser possible. Invest the maximum allowed in your retirement savings plan, and acquire income-producing assets that will help you and your family live more comfortably. Channel your purchases, too. Buy Black whenever you can. Recently I treated my family in Atlanta to massages and worked hard to find a Black-owned spa. I was referred to D'Lor Salon and Spa, an emporium in the Black community of Cascade and among the finest boutique spas I have visited anywhere. Every dollar you spend is an investment in how you want the world to work. Vote with your dollars.

Take your life back. Don't be held hostage by 24/7 connectivity, work and family demands, working like mules. Claim private time. Others respect us when we love and honor ourselves and ask for help when we need it. Without quiet time we become sad and sick. Work in as progressive an environment as possible, where output, not face time, is valued. Be an enlightened leader: Know that overworked, tired staff don't give their best and in time become disgruntled, depressed and ill. Break away from the pack. Less is more, and slower is faster. Your life awaits your attention and dedication.

*Complaint and compliance are not easier than taking action.*
*And why elect to ignore what we have the power to reinvent?*
*Your life needs your creativity, not your criticism.*

# our creative soul

There is an art to living well. Life itself is a work of art, and those who live it well do so creatively, artfully. But creativity is natural to every soul, not just to the people we call artists. Creativity goes beyond paint and canvas, dancing shoes, beads and string, needles and thread. Creativity is more basic and more deeply personal. It's particular, individual and placed in us by God so we can see clearly how to turn any situation to our advantage and shape the life we want at every level.

We are the heirs of people who have used the gift of creativity well—the make-a-way women in our families, the can-do men in our history. Necessity has always been the mother of invention.

Years ago, when I was a single mother raising my daughter, Shana, mounting credit card debt almost led to the loss of our apartment—and my sanity. But pain is always information; it's how life speaks to us when we're hardheaded. Feeling overwhelmed led me to create a new relationship with money and stop living beyond my means. I got a gig on the side by creating one: teaching models how to work their makeup and hair. I shuffled my priorities, which took some creativity, so I could make room to go to college and make my way out of the insecurity of being poorly educated. I gave my money worries some healthy, creative attention. I accepted the responsibility of managing my finances and my life more efficiently. I started getting up early each morning, eager to accomplish a day's work and excited about serving our community. Changing my mind and behavior and giving my time and energy back to the community unlocked the rewards of prosperity.

Our subconscious mind always seeks to protect and guide us. It would benefit us greatly to slow the pace, close the door on the world each day, and turn our attention to the One within. When we are relaxed and at peace, the wise voice is heard clearly and distinctly. I know this now, but life had to rough me up before I learned to respect and use God's great gift of creative intelligence every day of my life.

Join up with God, and you can creatively solve any personal problem. Then, when we all work together, we can solve the greater and graver ills around us. We can break the habit of settling for what we are presented with—illness, poverty, pain, war. Complaint and compliance are not easier than taking action. And why elect to ignore what we have the power to reinvent? Your life needs your creativity, not your criticism. Negative feelings, negative self-talk and a negative attitude all team up to dull our creative reflexes.

Each day, work at strengthening your faith. I feel powerful and fabulous after saying these truths aloud: "I'm like water, not stone, flexible and limber in my living and giving. I am healthy and happy. I learn things easily, and whatever I need to create my dreams rushes to meet me."

Say it with passion and conviction. You will train your subconscious mind to be open and optimistic, positive and poised to receive the fruits of the living spirit. God gave you richly all things to enjoy.

*Build wealth! Saving your lunch money—say, $10 a day—equals $300 a month. With 5 percent interest compounded over 40 years, it's $144,000. At 10 percent, you've got $1,897,224. Make that sandwich!*

# do the math

Which industry can Black folks claim financial ownership of? With all that our foreparents gave to build America's wealth, we as a people should be in a more powerful financial position, not sweating out our days on the work-and-spend treadmill, deep in debt.

Even if we're not sinking in debt today, our pensions and Social Security alone will barely sustain us in later years. But opportunity is always knocking; with active faith, we can open the door to prosperity. We can learn from financially independent people. We can learn to count.

Make it a mission to employ the magic of compounding, which makes millionaires and is as basic to wealth building as *ABC*'s are to reading and writing. The magic of compound interest is brilliantly illustrated in a story that tells how the emperor of China offered one wish to the inventor of the game of chess. The inventor replied that he wanted one grain of rice on square one of the chessboard, two grains on the second square, four on the third, and so on through square sixty-four. The unsuspecting emperor agreed to this seemingly humble request, but he didn't do the math. If the grains of rice on each square were doubled, the final one would require more than nine quintillion (a 9 followed by 18 zeroes) grains—more than all the rice in China.

The power of compounding applied to money over time can help us create the financial future we want. Just saving lunch money—say, $10 a day, equals to $300 a month—for 40 years would give us $144,000. But the same investment at 5 percent interest compounded annually over 40 years adds up to $457,806. Up the interest earned to 10 percent, and we'd end up with $1,897,224.

Volatility in the financial market demands that we have a diversified wealth-building plan that includes home ownership and a compounding retirement savings fund. And smartly investing in mutual funds as well as entrepreneurial efforts and real estate—perhaps with a partner—will help us pass along wealth, not debt, to our family. Working closely with a professional financial planner whose job it is to know investments and count our money with us, not for us, is a must.

Polish, presentation and quality brands are important to sisters. But those who plan to finish rich have awakened from the dream that more is better. They aren't about show; they've defined what enough is, and they save for what they want. They know that, above all things, it is God's wish that we prosper, that material wealth is but a reflection of the spiritual riches we must seek first and always.

Develop your own yardstick for what is valuable. Harvest happiness from the exquisite pleasures around you—the ever-changing sky, fresh flowers, the chatter of children at play. Before going to the checkout counter, consider the future and the financial cleavage in the Black community. Stand still for a moment and do the math.

*We sisters shouldn't still be struggling to make a good living or have a great life. We shouldn't be fighting the battles our foreparents already won. Only fools give up conquered ground.*

# it's about business

Earlier this decade, greed and dishonesty had caused a meltdown on Wall Street. All of us who had money in the market, in 401(k)s or in government or private pensions, saw our nest eggs dwindle and in some cases disappear. The boys at the top cheated, and we all got punished. Now the U.S. economy is in flux. While most of us aren't going to leave our jobs to become entrepreneurs, every one of us had better have a gig on the side, more than a single stream of income—real estate investments, a hobby turned into a business, a partnership, equity in a new venture. The only way to secure your future is to design it. Think business!

Money isn't meant to be our constant struggle. God puts in every one of our hearts and minds the ideas, passion and power we must have to prosper. Our job is to overcome the fear factor and become an open receptacle for God's gifts, which are always flowing our way.

Make the commitment today to create a more prosperous reality for yourself and for our people. We sisters shouldn't still be struggling to make a good living or have a great life. We shouldn't be fighting the battles our foreparents already won. Only fools give up conquered ground. We are the offspring of alpha women, sisters who reared and cared for Black and White America at once, all while building businesses and institutions that sustained the race. Even when Black people had little say-so in their lives and during times infinitely harsher than these, they were building on their own. And surely they had fears. But they moved forward anyway, not letting their fear override their faith.

Sarah Breedlove Walker certainly didn't. The single mother—my shero—was a washerwoman. She couldn't read or write. But she followed the vision she said God gave her to create beauty products for Black women. By 1916 Madame C.J. Walker had built her own manufacturing plant and employed 20,000 people throughout the Americas.

Mary McLeod Bethune, too, one of history's greatest educators, fought fear and won—for herself and us. In 1904 she started a school for little Black girls, which is today's Bethune-Cookman College. And she "marketed" her famously delicious sweet-potato pies to pay the school's monthly rent.

By 1920 Jamaican-born Marcus Garvey had organized the Black world. His Universal Negro Improvement Association connected people of African ancestry throughout the United States, the Caribbean, South and Central America, Europe and Africa. Under his leadership the UNIA bought a fleet of steamships, the Black Star Line, and provided food, housing and jobs to the poor. Without any of the technology at our fingertips today, Garvey linked Africans throughout the Diaspora and the Motherland, creating the largest and most successful mass movement of Black people in history. Marcus Garvey was a social entrepreneur, a role model for how we can build for-profit empires that fund the social needs of our people. His determination, innovative thinking and faith are proof that one bold and courageous spirit can have a positive impact on the world. Securing Black people and teaching us to love ourselves and do business among ourselves was his mandate.

*The saga of my grandmother's reckless trust and an experience with a lover, taught me a lesson no woman should forget: Never count on anyone but yourself to ensure your financial future.*

# wealth care

An older man of means I was crazy about in my twenties taught me a powerful lesson. Mr. J said I had no say-so in our relationship because I had no money. *Selfish*, I thought. *He's not the man I'll marry.* At home, on the money front, my mother had taught me about financial independence through her stories about her mother.

My grandmother worked hard, side by side with her lover in their lucrative numbers business; together they built their mini-empire in Harlem during the Depression—a couple of bars, liquor stores, a tailor shop and apartment houses. But my grandmother's life ended in poverty. After her man died, his children cut off her resources and put Mother out of her beautiful New Jersey home. Her name wasn't on the deed. Nor was it on any of the other holdings they had amassed.

The saga of my grandmother's reckless trust and my own experience with Mr. J taught me a lesson I have never forgotten: We must not depend on others to ensure our financial future. It is our responsibility alone.

Every time we incur debt we give away a piece of our future. To owe a creditor income we've not yet earned is a form of indentured servitude. African Americans have followed America's lead to fiscal irresponsibility, and we have this in common: great debt. We finance what we can't pay for and consume more than we produce. And just as America owns far fewer foreign assets than other countries own here, people foreign to our communities, to their credit and our shame, own more in our neighborhoods than we do.

Here are things we all can do to grow more powerful financially:

**Spend less than you earn.** Wealth is not determined by how much you make, but by how much you keep and grow.

**Value your time.** Your life is now; time is money. Don't waste a moment.

**Be strategic.** Talk with money-savvy people about asset building. Cut out idle chatter and mindless TV and use that time to read about building wealth and a retirement nest egg. Sign up for your company's 401(k) or other retirement plan. Tuck away $5 a day, and every 20 months you'll have saved $3,000.

**Hire yourself.** Create your lifestyle and a business around your passions, and work will never again feel like labor.

**Purchase property.** African Americans lag behind all other groups in home ownership, a major source of wealth in America. And it's the easiest, most sensible way for us sisters to amass assets that will cushion our elder years. Learn the real estate market in your area and begin building your portfolio of properties.

Like water, money flows through our hands. We can choose whether ours is drained or reserved for investment and growth. At the end of the day, we want more for our efforts than closets filled with clothes and shoes. Sisters, let's save lavishly and build wisely for the future; it will come whether we have the funds to live it well or not. Don't work for money, make money work for you.

*Because I wasn't prepared and took little care of my finances, I let $450,000 slip away. To create wealth, we need faith, a plan, expert advice—and to follow through.*

# a state of readiness

I moved into a tiny apartment in the middle of Manhattan when my Shana was five years old. Though I had to make the living room my bedroom, I felt lucky to live in the luxe tower with sweeping city views. Money was tight. I was parenting solo, and the $450 monthly rent was a stretch for me. We got into the building because the wealthy people it was built for didn't want to live in the area, which was still a bit seedy. But gentrification would soon come.

In a few years the building became a condominium, and the insider price for my apartment was $199,000. I didn't have a dime saved, and with my spotty credit there was no way I could qualify for a mortgage. So I remained a renter while my wealthy White neighbors snapped up apartments, sometimes combining two or three of them. Shana was a little girl when we moved in and married with a daughter when I moved out. Over the years the purchase price of my little apartment doubled, then tripled. By the time I left, the market value of my rented unit was $650,000.

My parents had struggled for years to buy a house for $10,000, which they still hadn't paid off a decade later when my father died. So I never imagined I could purchase an apartment that cost $199,000. But in retrospect, I see that I could have readied myself to do the deal. I knew far in advance that the building was going condo. I could have jumped off the work-and-spend treadmill, reordered my priorities, devised a strategy, put a financial plan in place. I could have gotten a second job, created a third income stream selling my popular home-baked coconut cookies. I could have developed a relationship with a Black bank in Harlem and made sure my credit was pristine. Instead I stayed stuck in the dispiriting rut of spending every dollar and planning not at all. I'd been given the gift of a beautiful apartment, but because my dreams were so small, I didn't prepare to receive the greater blessing, and $450,000 in increased property value slipped right through my fingers.

But our lessons are our greatest blessings, and this was a grand one for me. Often what holds us back, individually and as a community, is our lack of readiness: We need to have faith and a plan—and then to follow through.

Life is a game; we must know how to play it. And this is the most opportune time ever for Black women. We have talent, creativity, power. We are blessed. Ask God to show you what you should do next. Ask yourself, *What do I want? What shall I create? What will I give?* The answers always come. Pay attention to what you feel and see, and even to your dreams. Make a map, a detailed plan, and add the strategies to your daily to-do list. Prepare to succeed.

God is forever sending us what we need to make the most of ourselves. This is the promise of our birth, but we have to recognize and seize the opportunities. We have to show up. We have to be ready to do our part in fulfilling the promise.

# notes

Beloved Community

*Violence against women demoralizes us and eats into our psyches and self-esteem. We are creators, vessels, mothers. To permit attack at the level of creation is to destroy life at its source.*

# action, not silence

We've come so far—but the news is not all good. While some of us are doing fine, many are not. Violence, including sexual violence against Black women and girls, is a life-stunting reality, and our community has not taken strong and appropriate action. Grassroots and religious institutions, fraternal, sororal and civil-rights organizations have been conspicuously silent.

Yet ask in a gathering of women if any have been beaten by a partner or sexually abused, and most women in the room will speak up. I had relationships with two angry men in my twenties. In time, when they didn't get their way, a shout became a shove, then a slap, and we were at war. I went places I never want to go again, saw aspects of myself I don't want to own.

I fled both relationships with my daughter in my arms because I feared not only for my life but also for those men's lives. I'm not one to take a blow without retaliating.

There's an overrepresentation of Black women sentenced to life in prison. The vast majority of them resorted to homicide in answer to the brutality they encountered in their relationships. It's a well-documented fact that husbands, boyfriends and former lovers cause more injuries to women of every race than anything else, including accidents and muggings combined.

Violence—even the threat of it—has a deep and dehumanizing effect on society. It holds women prisoners—causes us to lose our sense of self and security. We may batter our children, do drugs or become suicidal. Violence in the lives of women demoralizes us and eats into our psyches and self-esteem. "Being female is life-threatening," says Charlotte Bunch, crusader against gender violence.

Our community has been a place of contradiction in the matter of protecting women. Black men risked life and limb to save us from being battered and raped by White men during slavery, which makes the brutalizing of sisters by brothers today all the more painful. I was hopeful that when White men who were sexually abused as children by pedophile priests began breaking their silence about their anguish, our community would courageously address the fact that the moral order has been broken among us too.

This is not only a women's issue: We all had a mother. And in his heart, no man wants to be a brute. Parents have to teach boys early on not to hit and make them see that by committing acts of violence, they not only wound others but also diminish themselves. Our organizations and our churches and temples, funded primarily by Black women, must have this conversation, which should also take place in every home, in every barbershop and beauty salon.

We women have to take steps to end our pain. Don't support artists whose lyrics and images degrade us, and don't accept verbal abuse, which is where physical violence begins.

We are creators, vessels, keepers of culture and community, mothers. To permit attack and degradation at the level of creation is to destroy life at its source.

Let's address this problem loud and strong. We are entitled to peace and protection, but we have to want this enough to expect it, to demand it and never stop shouting until it comes.

*The first rule of love is mindful listening, so I let my hands fall from my ears. The receptive door opened slowly. By morning I could see that I was pointing the finger but accepting none of the blame.*

# I apologize

The Combs and Taylor families have known each other for decades. Back in the day in Harlem, I was friends with Sean's parents, Janice and Melvin. When Janice and I became single mothers, we held our babies, Sean and Shana, near and grew closer. So "Godmommy" easily reached out to Sean in the midst of the storm raging about the defiling of Black women in rap culture. I asked Sean, innovator that he is, to take the lead in the hip-hop community and pledge not to produce lyrics or videos that devalue Black womanhood.

He responded that he had cleaned things up greatly on his Bad Boy label and invited me to listen to the music. Point! But I pushed back, and the e-mails flew between us. Our exchanges were intense, the generational tension high. "I feel everything you're saying," Sean countered. "But it's unfair to put all the pressure on rap music." He said that the hip-hop community was feeling the weight of my generation's hypocrisy, that rappers didn't invent bad behavior, and that it's in the company of our older men that boys learn disrespect and foul language.

I didn't want excuses. The bad boys of hip-hop are grown men today and know better. But the first rule of love is mindful listening, so I let my hands fall from my ears. Sean confessed that many of his generation believe we abandoned them. We left them to figure things out, he said, and they did the best they knew how. "Hip-hop has also given young people role models and opportunity," he argued. "We are producers, managers, accountants, lawyers, entrepreneurs. But we only hear from the elders when we mess up." And not in private, he lamented, but publicly on TV. "Y'all are going about this the wrong way," he declared.

"We need a hug, not another slap. When we are ready to sit together and tell the truth, that's when change will come."

Without honesty, there's no clarity or progress. After my exchange with Sean, the receptive door to deeper understanding opened slowly. By morning I could see that I was pointing the finger but accepting none of the responsibility. For that I apologize.

I apologize to our young people for my generation, for not governing the village more carefully, for not being more watchful over the influences we allowed into our children's lives. I apologize for letting misogyny and murderous messages become our refrain, poisoning our Black culture.

Black music propelled my generation forward: "Say it loud . . ." "Ain't no stoppin' us now. . ." Liberation music, love music, led us into the light. Yet when hip-hop was young, playful and political, parents dissed the music. When it turned vulgar and toxic, pimping vicious stereotypes of our people for profit, many of us called for censorship and government intervention instead of calling our children to account and counseling them in the ways of Black love and self-respect. It was our responsibility as parents to show them another way.

I apologize for dropping the baton, for my generation's not being more impassioned in sharing our history—what our foreparents withstood to open the doors we're walking through today. As an elder of the village, I take responsibility for allowing the poverty, crumbling communities and failing schools; they've given rise to the rage in rap and our state of emergency. And I promise there'll be no more naming and blaming.

Love corrects. Love directs. This is the function of the elders in our African tradition—to gather our children to us, heal our broken pieces, teach by force when necessary, but surely by example. Mindful listening and mutual activism are needed to secure our race. We all have learning to do.

*Let us not confuse the few symbols of the dream—trinkets that buy our silence—for the dream itself. Economic and social justice for all—shared progress—these are the goals.*

# the I that is we

The Caribbean beckons me. The spirit of the Motherland that traveled here with our ancestors calls me to remember who I am and what I'm supposed to be doing here. The African slave trade in the Caribbean, which began as a rivulet in 1501, became a torrent over the more than 300 years that it fueled Europe's economies. Our history lives in the islands my parents called home.

Recently I responded to the call. My overscheduled life was overtaking me, so I took a respite with my husband in an ideal spot for remembering and renewal: St. John in the U.S. Virgin Islands. At Caneel Bay, an earthy yet elegant resort nestled in the foothills of a national reserve—and far from the pressures of phones, faxes and e-mail—I slowed the pace and focused on what matters most.

Surrounded by the sapphire sea and lush, rolling hills, I could feel the presence of our ancestors, whose tortured lives were tied to the eighteenth-century sugar plantation where the resort now stands. I kissed the ground they walked and wept upon. I listened to their lives.

Eloquently and passionately, St. Johnians speak of history that's shared by Diaspora Africans—no matter where the slave ships left our foreparents. In St. John I heard and read historical accounts I will never forget.

In 1733 a bloody slave revolt took place against the Danish planters on the island's 109 plantations. It took English, Dutch and French reinforcements from neighboring islands seven months to put down the rebellion. The French commandant Longueville's eyewitness account tells how captured rebels were tortured to dissuade further rebellion: "One was burned to death slowly, another was sawed in half and the third impaled. The two Negro women had their hands and heads cut off after all five had been tortured with hot pincers." Mass suicides finally brought the rebellion to an end. Dear to oral tradition is the story of the men and women who climbed high onto a cliff called Mary's Point, held hands and jumped onto the jagged rocks, where their bodies were washed out to sea. St. Johnians' great-great-grands could still see the bloodstained rocks.

We've been taught European history so long that we've forgotten our own. We are the people whose faith and determination, whose commitment to mutual love and support have sustained us. I am because we are. And now how will we be? What will we middle-class African Americans—the most privileged people of African ancestry on the planet—do during our watch to help our sisters and brothers struggling along the margins? Let's not confuse the few symbols of the dream—material things that buy our silence—for the dream itself. We must keep the pressure on, keep pushing together until all of us have keys that open the door to the future. Economic and social justice, shared progress—these are the goals.

No one gets a pass; call yourself to account. Make staying healthy and keeping stress at bay top priorities. Then pick an issue that's inhibiting Black progress and work passionately for change.

In St. John I was reminded that our future is not at the mercy of external forces, no matter how mighty they may appear. Together we are the masters of our fate. One people, one power.

*Don't let education, income and status separate us. Those in the upper echelons are there to gain mastery and the power to create opportunities for more of us. The relationships we weave give us strength.*

# two worlds

An executive at a large communications company invited me to a presentation about the challenges facing the industry. When the meeting concluded, the only other African Americans present, two women, joined me to talk. I was stunned to discover that they were meeting for the first time. Both were new to the organization, worked on the same floor, had passed each other in the halls for weeks, but had never spoken. Each thought she was the only African American executive on the floor and that the other Black women were assistants.

Two Black women struggling to find their footing in a bastion of White-male power perpetuated their pain by failing to connect with each other and with their community—the veteran sisters who were administrative staff, who had survived several CEOs, mergers and downsizing and could have brought sunlight, support and strategy.

From the executive level to the mailroom, we are cut from the same cultural cloth. The relationships we weave give us strength. Those in the upper echelons are there to gain mastery and the power to create opportunities for more of us. Too often education, income and status separate us. But we are a bicultural people, living in two worlds, and must know the language and landscape of both.

W.E.B. DuBois wrote about our dual reality. We ever feel our "twoness," he said, two souls, two thoughts, two strivings, African and American, "always looking at one's self through the eyes of others," measuring ourselves against a world that doesn't consider us. His observations of a century ago hold true today, especially for the many of us who are in hierarchical, patriarchal, racist work environments.

But that old and dying order can't keep us from rising when we:

**Don our spiritual armor.** With daily spiritual focus you see the grand gifts that are always flowing from chaos.

**Get "prayed up" before leaving for work.** Ten minutes of spiritual practice will fortify you throughout pressured days.

**Have a plan.** Make your workplace your university, a stepping-stone to financial independence. Take development courses, ask questions. Reach forward for guidance and explanation of the culture, politics and unwritten policies and reach back to help others.

**Stay connected to the people.** Never underestimate the community work that brought us to these places of power. The National Urban League and NAACP need our support, and we need theirs. Lack of participation in our activist organizations costs us dearly. And the powers that be don't mess with you easily when you perform well and are connected to visible, valued community leadership.

With wisdom and strategy we'll stand confidently, our feet planted firmly in our double domain, proudly African and American, guided by the hand of God.

*Johnnie Cochran's politics didn't change with wealth and celebrity. He was working to win reparations for African Americans—wanted at least an apology from the government for enslaving us for 246 years.*

# Johnnie, we call your name

Johnnie Cochran left this life a hero. He was bold, brilliant, one of the sharpest legal minds ever. He loved Black people fiercely, was a freedom fighter, always on the move for us. How often we'd ask, "Where's Johnnie? I just saw him a moment ago." And where was Johnnie? Working for us. Saying "Hey!" to the cooks in the kitchen. Or talking to folks on the street. Johnnie invested himself in the community.

Celebrities in trouble had him on speed dial: Michael Jackson, Sean Combs, Football Hall of Fame's Jim Brown, former child star Todd Bridges. As the lead attorney on O.J. Simpson's defense team, Johnnie Cochran became one of the most recognizable people in the world, a daily guest in all our living rooms. But much of his 42-year career as a lawyer was dedicated to fighting institutional racism and injustice: He fought for three decades to win freedom for Geronimo Pratt, a Black Panther Party member who was wrongly convicted of murder.

Johnnie Cochran's politics didn't change with wealth and celebrity. He was working to win reparations for African Americans. He wanted at least an apology from the government for enslaving us for 246 years. Johnnie represented hundreds of victims of racial profiling and police brutality: In New York City, Abner Louima was beaten and sodomized with the wooden handle of a toilet plunger by cops, and Amadou Diallo, innocent and unarmed, died in a hail of 41 police bullets.

Johnnie represented the family of Cynthia Wiggins, a young mother in upstate New York who was crushed to death by a truck while trying to cross a busy thoroughfare. Cynthia had to cross the heavily trafficked road to get to her part-time job at an upscale mall because buses from her Black community weren't permitted to pull up in front of the mall like those ferrying White shoppers.

Johnnie stood for the four young men stopped by state troopers on the New Jersey Turnpike for driving while Black. They were on their way to North Carolina Central University to try out for basketball scholarships. When the nervous driver tried to put the van in park and it slipped into reverse, the troopers opened fire. Bleeding from multiple gunshot wounds, the young men were pulled from the van, handcuffed, strip-searched and made to lie facedown in a gully. A search of the van turned up a Steinbeck novel and a Bible.

Johnnie Cochran gave us a glimpse of what our ancestors fought so hard for, what so many died for, what so many of us thought we would never see: JUSTICE.

The verdict is in. Johnnie has been set free. And for any who may still be wondering, *Where's Johnnie gone now?* He's here, conjured up in a million memories, walking around in the recollections of his wife, Dale, who cared for him till his last breath, and in all of us who remember.

There's a West African proverb that says as long as you call a person's name, his spirit lives. Hey, Johnnie! Love you, brother! Thank you, beloved. In the end there was little of you left for death to claim. Death got cheated because we got it all.

*The profit-making prison system is devouring our young. More than a million Black males are now incarcerated in the U.S. Oh, hell no! We are not going down like this. What is sacred to us if not our children?*

# 17 teardrops

When I met first Robinette, she was a troubled teen wrestling with life. The child of a drug-addicted mother, Robinette had dropped out of school and was fighting to save her little sister, who was floundering in foster care. A friend of mine who is an educator helped get Robinette into a high school just blocks from the *Essence* offices, and after class she would come to work with me. My assistant, Debra Parker, and I did what we could to help sweet Robinette move toward positive self-regard and the rewards of self-regulating behavior. It was a joy to see her take control of her life and blossom.

Today Robinette is twenty-five, a capable young woman and a home owner. She is working to return to college and was engaged to be married. But last fall, Robinette and her fiancé were walking down a Harlem street, hugged up, when the unthinkable happened. While holding on to her, Robinette's beloved was shot in the head and killed. She remembers his pushing her out of the way to safety. The shooter was aiming at another brother but missed his mark, shattering Robinette's heart and her happiness.

Gathered at my home one evening, my niece Sahara, Robinette's sister Jaynea, attorney Aishaah Rasul and I held Robinette close, to support and console her. We heard her sad truth: "Everyone I love, I lose," she whispered. "My mother, both my grandmothers, now Nathaniel. For the first time in my life I had some joy, but now it's gone."

This tragic story is not unique. That evening, Aishaah recounted a situation that shocked me into silence. She described a young man she'd met in prison who had teardrops tattooed on his face. Seventeen of them. Each tattoo brought him honor in his gang; each was a symbol of a life he had taken, a record of another brother he'd gunned down. For every teardrop, for every life taken, on purpose or by mistake, there are hundreds of broken hearts. Love and life are erased in the time it takes to raise a hand, pull a trigger, hit or miss.

Black love has grown cold. Look at what we've allowed: A third of Black children are poor. Schools are failing them. More than half of all Black fourth graders are functionally illiterate. The criminal-justice system is devouring our young; a reprehensible educational system is feeding them into the pipeline of an unjust, for-profit prison system that has just hit a new and hideous high: Nearly 2 million Black males are now incarcerated in the United States.

Oh, hell no! We are not going down like this. What is sacred to us if not our children? What success will we have without our successors? We must come together to implement a plan to right our upside-down sense of what's important. In July 2006, when we held The Essence Music Festival in Houston because Hurricane Katrina kept us from being at home in New Orleans, we put out the call for the *Essence* Cares Campaign. Oprah Winfrey reissued the call to action during an inspiring show focused on solving the crisis among our young, and we continued that call when we went home to the Crescent City in July 2007. This is what we are asking: that every able, stable Black man and woman place a guiding hand on a vulnerable young person's shoulder and mentor that youngster to wholeness and high achievement.

Think about it. If we knew there was one thing—just one thing—we could do to roll back the numbers of our babies dropping out of school, being dropped into prison, or worse, wouldn't we do it? In some cities, only 18 percent of Black boys are graduating from high school. Nearly 7 percent of Black babies are born to girls under 18.

Well, every available statistic tells us that mentoring works magic. Mentored children are much less likely to skip school, abuse alcohol or take drugs. Even youngsters in deep crisis become more hopeful and positively energized when a caring adult enters their lives.

One of my six mentees, who was 15 years old and incarcerated when I met her, just graduated from college at the top of her class and is off to grad school. And I didn't do much. I just took her along with me to meetings and some speaking engagements, so she could see a wider world, and encouraged her to get her G.E.D. I told her to have fun with the fellas, but no matter how they beg and plead, or how turned on she feels, "Do not have sex."

Mentoring costs nothing and doesn't require a lot of time. Mentoring works miracles. The commitment to help is the medicine, the herb, the healing potion needed to rescue a generation. In Atlanta alone, 2,000 boys are on the local Big Brothers Big Sisters waiting list, hoping that caring and compassionate "Bigs" will show up and sign up to mentor them.

Just as girls need big sisters and mothers to stand with them, so, too, our boys need solid grown-up men in their lives—role models who look like them and who will help guide them to manhood.

# notes

# notes

# Undying Love

*The pain of losing a loved one is a powerful reminder of how blessed we are to have loved, and how important it is not to wait to bring the fullness of our love to every now moment.*

# transition

When my mother died, I thought I'd never stop crying. For the first time I understood the profound sense of loss my daughter's godmother, Trish Ramsay, had expressed when her mother passed away the previous year. I had flown to Jamaica to be with my Trishy, and as we clung to each other among the thousands of happy travelers moving around us at Norman Manley Airport, she spoke of what now seemed to her like inadequate expressions of sympathy—the cards, the hugs, the pats on the back—she had given to friends who'd lost their mother. Until she lost her own, she confided, she'd had no sense of the depth of sorrow and utter despair they must have been feeling. "I feel so alone," she sobbed in my arms. "Now I have no one to pray for me, to intercede for me, no one between me and God."

Neither of our parents died prematurely. Both were in their early eighties and had lived long and fruitful lives. Yet, no matter how old or ill our parents are, we don't want them to leave; but when the spirit is ready to return home to Spirit, it takes flight, whether the flesh is nine or ninety.

Scientists now know that energy and matter are not created or destroyed, only transformed from one state into another. There is no loss in the universe. My mother's transition taught me that truth. And although my beloved Babs's death was staggeringly painful, it gave me the gift of a richer, more meaningful life.

Note: This essay is adapted from my book *Lessons in Living*

During the nine months she lay ailing, I was able to hug and hold her the way I'd always wanted her to embrace me. I was able to nurture her, to caress her and tell her how much I cherished her. Mommy was not at all demonstrative and would never have permitted that show of love and tenderness had she been alert and strong. Like my father (who had made his transition twenty years earlier, ten months before my Shana was born), she was uncomfortable with displays of affection. She had been a housewife all her life; her days revolved around her family. She took perfect care of her children, but always seemed distant and sad.

By the time my mother's health began to slip, I had come to terms with not having the warm and intimate relationships with her I'd hungered for since I was a little girl. My healing had begun years before when, as she aged, she more willingly shared some of her most private truths. I urged Babs to talk to me about her life, about the secret hurts and unrealized dreams that so many women of her generation tuck away but do not forget. I discovered that beneath Mommy's stoic demeanor lay a heart that had yearned for a fuller life—she'd longed to work outside the home, to have her own money, to travel, to have free-roaming conversations with women friends and a greater involvement with the world. But my Trinidadian mother had married a reclusive man.

My father was born in 1898 on the sleepy little Caribbean island of St. Kitts, worlds away from the social clamor of Harlem. Lawrence was a quiet, stern and fiercely private man. He'd married late in life, was a good provider for his family, but was emotionally closed. When I was growing up, no friend of his ever visited our household except for Mrs. Gibbs, with whom he played the numbers each weekday morning. No friends of my parents ever came to dinner. I'd always thought that was also my mother's choice, but so many years later, when she shared her recollections with me, I learned that she had felt as stifled and isolated as I had at times.

In learning what had disheartened Babs, I was freed from taking her coolness personally. I also began to see that too often we expect mothers to love us in exactly the way we want to be loved, and want them to accept our love in exactly the way we want to give it.

After a second stroke, my mother lost most of her mobility. I had been making plans to bring her back to the family home when, during a meeting with the social worker at the rehabilitation institute where Babs had spent several months in therapy, I had to reconsider. We were going over the renovations that would have to be made to accommodate my mother's wheelchair when the social worker realized that, given the configuration of the Harlem brownstone, in the event of a fire my mother would be trapped. I was digesting the discouraging new information when my sister, Lillian, and my daughter, Shana—each had an apartment in the building—put their arms around me and asked that I step out of the office. They reminded me of the many arduous days at home after Mommy's first major stroke, days when her caregivers were late or didn't show up at all. They pointed out that Moms was still mentally alert then and through therapy had regained the ability to walk. The situation was far different now. Although her devoted physician, Dr. Cordia Beverley, had worked passionately and aggressively to rehabilitate her, my mother remained confined to a wheelchair, her mind lost in the past.

Over the years, whenever I'd taken her to visit her aging friends in nursing homes, I'd promised myself that my mother would never end up in such a place—that she would always be cared for at home. Now I was forced to learn a difficult lesson: Never say never.

Although our hearts were breaking, my brother, Larry, Lillian and I quickly set about finding the best nursing home for our mother. After interviewing knowledgeable health-care workers and friends who had faced similar challenges, and after visiting several sites, we decided on a small nursing home just a mile north of my apartment. We were grateful to learn that Babs would share a large airy room with three other women. Her bed would be next to a window that looked out on Riverside Park and the Hudson River.

*God is so good*, I was reminded throughout this sad and challenging time. Once again I could see clearly how the Creator works through us. When we make a decision and try our best to do the right thing and keep moving forward, Spirit opens the way. Everything needed for Babs to get settled into her new home had fallen smoothly into place.

My mother had even assisted: In the years before she became ill, when her body was still healthy and her mind strong, Babs would periodically call us to sit with her and review her personal papers. Invariably we'd resist, insisting that she'd be around for a long time to come. But she would tell us that we were being foolish. "I've got to die sometime," she'd declare, "and I don't want any confusion when I'm gone. Now come, sit yourselves down and let me tell you what's what."

Wisely, she had recognized the inevitable; Moms had made peace with the one thing her children couldn't bear to admit—that she would one day make her transition. So when the time came for us to take her affairs in hand, we knew precisely where every document was and what we needed to do.

Thank God for my mother's foresight. A second stroke weakened her body and her will. It was then that Mommy started traveling back in time and, for the first time in my recollection, seemed truly happy and at ease.

Each time I visited, she greeted me with loving, smiling eyes and outstretched arms. I was like a sponge. I wanted to be with my mother every possible moment, to absorb her new openheartedness.

Sadly, two months after her arrival at the nursing home, Mommy had a devastating seizure that left her bedridden and unable to talk. A nursing-home doctor told me there was nothing more they could do for her and that she could pass away any day. As I stood at her bedside, I thought: *There lies the woman who put her life, her happiness on hold for me.*

Babs had made the sacrifice I wouldn't have made: She'd stayed in a confining marriage so that she could raise her children without disrupting our lives. I'd seen Mommy put cardboard in her worn-out shoes so that we could have new ones. She had converted to Catholicism and pinched money from the cash register in Daddy's clothing store to give us the best education available in our Harlem neighborhood—at the local Catholic school. Now, watching her lying in bed, defenseless and unresponsive, I refused to accept the finality of the doctor's words. I refused to give up hope. I was determined to prolong my mother's life and to make her as comfortable as possible.

In the months that followed, I learned many lessons about bringing comfort to our loved ones and helping them make a smooth transition. In the past, when I'd visited my mother or friends in the hospital, I had sometimes accused the nurses and aides of being curt and insensitive. Now that I was spending hours each day at the nursing home, I could see that the caregivers had too much to do, and that there were too few of them. But during the months that Babs was moved back and forth between the nursing home and the hospital, I discovered that patient care improves when it becomes obvious that loved ones are involved and monitoring the care.

Babs had become immobile and incontinent. I didn't want her to get bedsores or a rash from soiled diapers, so I requested that the staff change and turn her from side to side more frequently throughout the day. If I thought someone wasn't handling my mother gently, I would ask that person kindly to "Please treat my beloved with the same reverence with which you would want me to treat yours."

At first the nursing staff resisted my efforts to help them with my mother, but in time they accepted me as a partner in her care. I kept my own stock of surgical gloves, wipes and creams at her bedside and learned how to wash her and change her gown and the bed sheets, how to turn her and exercise her limbs. During this time I often recalled the riddle of the Sphinx, which my mother quoted frequently as she grew older and felt the frustration of her memory and agility beginning to fail: "Once a man, twice a child." It was now true: Babs had become my baby.

Every experience serves to focus us on the meaning of life, and nothing does that more than facing our own mortality or the imminent passing of a loved one. Although I wasn't aware of it at the time, while I was caring for my mother I was learning an important life ritual that isn't taught in our youth-oriented society: By helping my mother through her transition, I was adding a new dimension to my life; I was unconsciously evoking and celebrating the spiritual connection that exists between mothers and daughters. In retrospect, the ritual I was practicing felt like the most loving and natural thing to do, a variation on the rituals our foremothers had adopted centuries before to assist their loved ones in making the transition. I saw my place in the continuum.

Lillian brought our mother's rosary beads and picture of Jesus from home and hung them on the wall near her bed. We placed our family portrait on her nightstand. Although she seemed to have lost her vision by then, the photograph symbolized the fruits of her life's labor and reminded the hospital staff that she was part of a loving family. A glass of water, the elixir of life, was always at her bedside. We kept fresh flowers on the windowsill and placed a small tape player near her so that she could listen to her favorite music throughout the day. Babs particularly loved the sweet sounds of Nat "King" Cole and soothing spirituals sung by Jessye Norman and Kathleen Battle.

During this period I reached out to a network of holistic healers in Manhattan: Daya, Dr. Ronald Davidson and Dr. Jifunza Wright. Any advice they offered that felt intuitively right to me became part of the ritual. I was allowed to take Babs off the liquid food supplement the caregivers had been feeding her through a tube and replace it with a mixture of Chinese herbs, spirulina (a protein-and-nutrient–rich algae) and fresh vegetable and fruit juices. Babs responded well and for a short time even began eating solid food again.

Healer Asar Ha-Pi, who lives in Chicago and teaches an ancient form of Egyptian yoga, shared some massage techniques he had used to comfort his father through his transition. He suggested I massage my mother's temples and feet with olive oil each day. This became my cherished daily ritual. I enjoyed the feeling of intimacy and closeness that arose from being able to comfort her. I extended my massages to include her face, neck, arms and legs, and I whispered her favorite prayers to her during this treasured time. It gave me great pleasure to dab soothing and familiar fragrances under Mommy's nose. I knew that lavender, gardenia and bay rum—the fresh, spicy scent that many older Caribbean people are so fond of—would please her.

Much to the doctors' amazement, Babs was still clinging to life months after they thought she would have been long gone. When Trish, who in her twenties had been a nurse, flew up from Jamaica for a visit, she helped me see that my mother was suffering and possibly holding on to life for me. Trish gently suggested that I release Babs, that I tell her it was all right to leave. I remembered what my mother had often said: "Death is not a punishment, but a resting place for the weary."

A week after Trish returned to Jamaica, I followed her advice. Mommy was struggling so. I whispered to her that I now felt capable and strong, that I would have her spirit with me always and it was all right to let her physical body go. I draped a piece of kente cloth on top of her covers. The rich, colorful cloth, woven over the centuries by the Ashanti of Ghana, symbolized that a faithful daughter, a queen, was going home. I promised my mother I'd keep the family together and wear the mantle that she and her mother and grands had worn so proudly and well.

A few days later, my mother made her transition. After her spirit left, I prayed over her body, holding her hand. I had never seen such stillness; it was never more evident to me that life is breath, not flesh. My mother's body lay in the bed, but my beloved Babs had gone home.

Death, as with life, is part of God's plan; it is a natural transition from life as we know it—a passage we all must face, but which our society treats as a great taboo. We are seldom encouraged to accept our mortality, and we're offered little help in dealing with the anguish of losing a loved one. But we would be much less anxious about our own eventual transition, and much more sensitive and supportive of those we love who are ailing and aged, if our view of life included the inevitability of death.

I will be forever grateful that after our stormy decades, I had many years to show my mother my gratitude for the sacrifices she'd made for me. I am one of the lucky ones: I had the chance to bid my mother farewell. I meet so many throughout the country who are not so fortunate, whose loved ones have died suddenly and out of season.

Grief is a natural response to the death of a loved one, and an important part of the healing process. But we have to acknowledge the pain before the healing can begin. Unexpressed grief can be destructive. It can make us intensely angry, fearful of intimacy and dependent on substances that dull or mask our pain, which will lead to other emotional problems. We should draw near to friends with whom we feel comfortable and comforted talking about our loss.

One of the most helpful things we can do for someone who is grieving is to stay in touch. It often happens that within a week following the funeral, people seem to forget about the bereaved and that the person left behind is still in a lot of pain. Remember to give a friend who is in mourning a call each day. Check in, see how the person is doing. We can be of great comfort to grieving hearts simply by lending an ear.

If we are the one suffering and are having difficulty coping with the loss and moving on with our life, we should reach out for help. We should join a grief-recovery support group or talk to a minister or a therapist. Above all, we can ask God to heal our heart. The pain of losing a loved one is also a powerful reminder of how blessed we are to have loved, and how important it is to not wait to bring the fullness of our love to every now moment.

# notes

# notes

onversations

# heart stuff, with Ruby Dee

I have adored Ruby Dee for decades and was passionate about having an intimate conversation with her. The life of Ruby Dee, a wisdom warrior, has been a treasure trove of experience: as a gifted award-winning actress, writer, producer, activist; as mother of three wonderful children and grandmother of seven; as a partner in a 56-year marriage to the phenomenal Ossie Davis, who died in February 2005 and was crazy in love with her.

Share tender moments with us as Miss Ruby talks about success and difficulty, about long-term love and partnership, and about how deeply she misses Ossie. This is an excerpt from the conversation we had for many hours four months after her beloved Ossie passed away.

*Miss Ruby, you've been so courageous and way ahead of your time. You pursued a career that took you away from your family in an era when absolute dedication to the home was demanded and expected of women. How did you find the courage to claim the freedom that most men take for granted but women don't?*

I never really had that freedom and I felt envious of what I thought was the male prerogative. In the beginning of our marriage, Ossie would come home, sit down, kick off his shoes, and read the paper while I struggled with the dinner, the dishes and the babies. I was resentful knowing that he'd get another acting job, be around all these exciting people, and leave me with all the real work. But that resentment faded as we began to work out the details of our marriage. Ossie started pitching in and trying so hard to please me. He became an active husband, and he began to include me more when he got a job. He'd ask if there was a part for me. And when I got a job and he wasn't working, he'd say, "I'll stay here and take care of the children." Sometimes he'd say, "I'll go with you," and we'd take the children along. Ossie was marvelous with the children. He'd get up in the middle of the night to bring the babies to me for feedings, he'd wash diapers and take the children out on Sundays to give me a break.

*You admit to being plagued by fuzzy thoughts and doubts about your strengths. But still you've been a brave explorer and have achieved so much. How do you push through doubt and fear?*

The worries and fears about personal lacks are immobilizing and make me dream the dream too long. But the dreams stay in my head, they haunt me, they push me and become a kick to my consciousness, making me act. The Divine Impulse—it's always safe to follow it. We've got to trust it and go wherever it takes us. Especially women. We women have a great function to perform. The world needs us. Feminine sensibilities are not being acknowledged, and we've allowed the antipeople to steal the children and are tolerating far too much: the assault on ourselves, the families of the world, permitting war and rape. More women are becoming enraged about these things and I think we're on the verge of doing something about them.

*I see that, too—women creating more humane societies as we discover our wisdom and courage and learn to trust using our feminine powers more fully. Was it difficult for you to cut out the superfluous in order to cultivate the things that you really wanted and that mattered most to you?*

Yes. And I haven't totally succeeded. My constant battle is putting aside time wasters, and I have to watch out for procrastination. Staying on the path of something you're trying to create has much to do with having confidence in yourself and in your capacity to realize the things you want out of life.

*Do you think we have a moral assignment?*

Yes. Ossie would speak about this frequently. We have to bring forward the graces in life and make them real. We have to institute democracy, which is still mostly an aspiration, and universal love, which is still unrealized. I dream of getting prisons off the stock exchange. It is a dastardly crime and an insult to the word *democracy* to make a commodity of jailing people.

*The Dee-Davis union is a way shower for our community. But no couple can be married for 56 years without rough spots. Did you and Ossie have any hurdles you thought you wouldn't be able to overcome?*

Yes—it was Ossie's not wanting anything. I knew that once he had lived out-doors because he couldn't pay his rent. He was a creature of the earth, and he didn't worry about things like that, because he felt he was always going to have a place to stay and something to eat. That used to gall me, because I was a worrier. He'd say, "I'll think about so-and-so when we need money for some-thing, but damned if I'm going to worry about it." And true enough, some-thing would happen, and we'd always come out of the difficult times.

*You had blowups, but did you ever break up?*

I threatened to leave him once, and the next day he said to me, "Well, if you ever decide to go and marry somebody else, just tell him to make a space for me, because I'm coming with you." Ossie always had something funny to say about everything. We had marvelous arguments. I learned that if I stuck to my guns, when I was right he'd come back to me sometimes and improve on my argument to him. We had no unusual salvation from the problems of other couples—we fought about family, money, ruined business, infidelity. We had terrible fights. But there was never anything that happened, no matter how incredible it might seem, that we didn't forgive each other for or agree to let go. Ossie and I both finally understood that there wasn't any reason we could come up with ever to leave each other.

*In your book* **With Ossie and Ruby,** *you both discussed having had what was called an open marriage for a short time during the 1960's. You allowed each other to have outside lovers. That's a huge leap for Black folks.*

Ossie couldn't lie. He refused to lie. He felt strongly that extramarital sex didn't destroy marriages, but that lies and deception did. Of course this was before AIDS and at a time when ideas about sex and marriage were changing rapidly. We both understood that there were absolutely marvelous, beautiful people in the world, that there were temptations to be with them, and that we two weren't the only ones we'd be attracted to. So we gave ourselves permission to have other partners if we wished to, as long as we were honest, kept it private, and didn't expose the family to scandal or disease. Ossie prided himself on not being a jealous person. "The most miserable thing," he would say, "is to love and not trust." And he was such a loving and giving person. Not just to me and not just in a romantic sense.

*How did this period in your marriage end?*

It didn't last long, and when Ossie put an end to it, I was glad it was over. He saw that it could hurt many people and break up families. It's too dangerous; you could come upon somebody you couldn't let go of. We saw that what you treasure most could be lost. And Ossie and I had matured. We began to understand that it is possible to be married to one person and be faithful to that person all your life, and that in a marriage loyalty and fidelity and trust cannot be compromised.

*Any regrets?*

If there is anything I could ask forgiveness for, it is this.

*What do you think Ossie would say to brothers today about infidelity?*

I think he'd say that no matter what you may feel for someone outside your marriage, he realized that you can't mess up your family, you can't mess around with love because there are serious consequences. There really is no such thing as an innocent affair. Preserving the family means everything to our community now. One of Ossie's sayings was, "You can rise no higher than where you have your feet planted in the community."

*At this tender time, what would you say it was that made the fullness and longevity of your relationship with Ossie possible?*

The fact that we worked together, thought a lot alike, and came from the same background. Ossie, his soil was the South, in Waycross, Georgia; mine was the North, in Harlem. But we both came from like soil in different places. And we both loved words and ideas. Some of our best times were just talking to each other, and as we got older, we talked about everything. There was nothing we couldn't tell each other, nothing too private for us to share.

*What advice would you give to us sisters and brothers that will help us walk the long road together?*

Get to know each other as human beings. Black women have to know the historical and everyday struggles of Black men, and our men have to know the struggles of Black women in America. Even before I knew Ossie, even before we fell in love, I knew the man, because I knew the situation of Black people. You have to help each other know who you are. You have to sanction each other's gifts and encourage each other. "I want you to be the best you were put here on this earth to be, even if it costs me," Ossie would say, and he lived it. He told me on so many occasions, "I love you means I want you to be the best you can be, whether it benefits me or not."

*How does it feel to have loved so deeply for so long and to have been loved so deeply in return?*
I have an incredible feeling of thanksgiving. When I feel like complaining, I remember how blessed I am to have been married to Ossie. I miss him incredibly, especially in the mornings. He would get up early and read the papers and discuss it all with me over breakfast. At night he'd wait for me to come to bed and sometimes I'd be messing around, doing this and that, and by the time I got to bed, he'd be asleep. I'm so sorry I didn't hurry up. We just loved being together. When I wasn't working, I started going to work with him. I'd visit the set, and it was great being in hotels together. It was like our little honeymoon.

*Did you know he was leaving?*
I knew because I could see him wasting away. He had a pacemaker and only one kidney, and his breathing was being affected. I think it was his heart. I do miss him so, I can't tell you. I still have him upstairs; Ossie was cremated. He just wanted an urn big enough for both of us.

*What will you have inscribed on the urn?*
"We're in this thing together." Ossie made that up.

# courage to love, with Cornel West

Cornel West—scholar, activist, writer, preacher, teacher—sat down with me in New Orleans during The Essence Music Festival, which we have held in the city's Superdome and Convention Center over the July Fourth weekend since 1995. The professor and I spoke about Black men's and women's pressing need to love one another more fully.

We had our conversation in a place where Black love would be all that would hold us together after the city and the Gulf were deluged and left with mass devastation, death and despair.

The horror the world watched unfold in New Orleans in the wake of Hurricane Katrina was, as Brother West said, "the most naked manifestation of conservative social policy toward the poor, where the message for decades has been: 'You're on your own.'" Poor Black people's humanity, he added, has been rendered invisible, so they were not a high priority once the affluent had gotten out and the helicopters came for the few; most of the people stuck on rooftops and in shelters and left to die on the side of the road were poor and Black. "From slave ships to the Superdome was not that big a journey," he observed.

The Black middle class now has an even greater obligation, Cornel West said, to actively love the 33 percent of Black children living in poverty and to fight for them. And "now that the aid is pouring in, vital as it is," he cautioned, "do not confuse charity with justice. I'm not asking for a revolution. I am asking for reform. A Marshall Plan for the South could be the first step."

Here, the month before the storm, is our conversation at the Convention Center in 2005 about how we sisters and brothers can love one another more strongly and stand together on solid ground:

*Brother Cornel, throughout our history here, Black love has been under siege: We don't fully understand how 250 years of slavery along with continuing racism and oppression have deeply fractured our lives and relationships. Our young suffer in underserved schools and are corralled into prisons; disparities in health care, housing and employment cripple us. But strong partnerships will strengthen us so no forces arrayed against us can win. How can we create healthy, lasting relationships?*

You don't learn how to love without being courageous and free. The challenge for us brothers has been mustering the courage to really look at ourselves, examine ourselves and find out who we really are. In a certain sense this means learning how to die and allowing a new self to emerge. This is important in all relationships and necessary if we are to love in a substantive way. If you're the same self you were before the relationship, you haven't loved deeply enough.

*This is a difficult task given that Black culture and this society don't encourage emotional honesty, intimacy or self-love in men. So how do we begin to shift? How can brothers like you encourage more men to be who they truly are and be true to their emotional selves?*

We have to form fellowships and networks of brothers who are trying to exemplify the courage to love. But courage is relatively sparse; people who want to be free are always a small group. Most would rather languish in conformity, complacency and even cowardice. But what is life for but to learn to love and be free and courageous?

*Are you brothers having these very critical discussions among yourselves?*

Absolutely! And the conversations are rich, because we have to be vulnerable. We have to be willing to be emotionally naked and to risk showing aspects of ourselves that we're not always proud of. But the fellowship helps us overcome the fear we have of facing ourselves.

### Is it difficult to be emotionally naked with women?

Yes. We brothers here in America wrestle with a profound rage. We have to be on the defensive all the time and ready for the next insult or assault. So it feels much more natural to pose and posture. When you're on the defensive all the time, it's very difficult to risk opening yourself and being vulnerable. But at the same time you say to yourself, I can't go through life in this posing posture without really loving or knowing what it's like to be free, because I'll never know me.

### What is it we women need to know about the interior lives of our men that is difficult for them to articulate?

I think a number of sisters already know, because you have studied the brothers, loved the brothers, reflected on the brothers—sometimes more than the brothers have reflected on themselves. But the major thing to know is how a mature response to the profound rage can be enacted and that it takes the form of a certain kind of love manifesting, both affirmation and acknowledgement, but also loving correction. Because it's so easy for us brothers to manipulate sisters' patience, as the sisters attune to our rage. If a woman is too patient or even too submissive and deferential, she easily becomes an object of manipulation.

So we want sisters to acknowledge the rage, but we also need love, patience and correction. It's the only way we will grow. Some brothers are denying the rage, the way America wants to deny the source of the rage, which is racism.

*Many Black women are tired, disappointed and hurt. Some have run out of patience and have given up. Sisters want respect and fidelity, help with finances, chores and caring for the children. What can Black women do to build the supportive and self-respecting partnerships they deserve without sacrificing themselves?*

The patience I'm talking about goes hand in hand with the willingness to be tender, to be sweet and kind without being manipulated by brothers. You want to do it in such a way that you still preserve your own sense of self, preserve your own integrity. Because both of us—men and women—are wounded. And I think in life the fundamental question is whether you choose to be a wounded hurter or a wounded healer. And choosing to be a wounded healer is always difficult, but it is spiritually mature, morally correct, and in the end the most rewarding.

*Women feel most deeply wounded when we are betrayed by infidelity. Infidelity has dissolved as many relationships as economic pressures have, and this situation is having a disastrous impact on Black families. Is it just all about sex? Do some men just want multiple partners, or is infidelity driven by a hunger and a longing for something deeper that men and women need to understand?*

I think it's both. On the one hand there's a certain kind of greed, a sense of wanting everything, having one's cake and eating it too. The whole culture sends the message—through the mass media and advertising—that you can have it all. But what they're talking about is pleasure. They're not talking about joy. They're not talking about what you experience when you look into the eyes of your child, your mother, your loved one, your valued one. The one who will be there when you're in a wheelchair or in the hospital with you when you're down and out. That's the joy that is pushed to the background.

We're bombarded with the need to have pleasure, which encourages greed and a self that's without constraint.

But on a deeper level, compulsive sexual behavior does bespeak a certain void that many of us brothers have. And we have a fear of dealing with the void, because it will require much more than just going to the next club or getting the next phone number. You're going to have to truly deal with people you love, and change your life. You really have to have someone who you can be honest, candid and open with or you'll end up drifting. Our relationships have to be substantive. If you just settle for what is slightly enough, sooner or later you'll start questioning why you're with this person.

*My husband, Khephra, says so often that our great need is for brothers to grow up, mature and take responsibility for their relationships. Securing our children and recovering our communities demand that we all make major changes in our lives and in our relationships.*

Historically, for Black people, religion has played an important role in getting us to think about changing our lives. Jesus changed many a Negro's life; I can testify to that myself. This is not to say that the church isn't flawed as an institution, and leadership needs to meet a lot of challenges. But there is no doubt that religion has made a lot of Black people examine themselves, put restraints on themselves, and become more responsible and accountable to something outside their egos. The breaking down of narcissism—that's very much what we're talking about: the greed of the self and the void that is still there, that narcissism doesn't even fill. It's after your hundred-and-fifth affair and you're still lonely—it's time to check yourself. Something is wrong.

*Video images and messages in the music that degrade Black women are having a tremendously negative impact on our community—glorifying pimp life, portraying*

ALL ABOUT LOVE

242

*our young women as disposable sexual objects, and encouraging young men to be players forever, instead of even trying to mature. We seem so far away from our needed cultural shift.*

We have to be real enough to tell the truth, to talk about the consequences of being a player, that in the face of death, dread and disappointment, the playing won't fill the void that you have to come to terms with and that it's actually going to reinforce it. If your mother dies, the strip club won't provide the resources to deal with that loss. But we do see folks in hip-hop culture undergoing changes. For all we know, 50 Cent may end up a freedom fighter in the tradition of Malcolm, after certain kinds of experiences.

*You've been married three times, and now you're single. What have you learned from those unions?*

I've learned that I need to confront my own fears and anxieties more candidly so that I really know who I am. So what I bring to the table is not looking for someone to fill my void, so that I'm not looking outward to find fulfillment, but already have a certain sense of it I can share with another. This takes a tremendous level of spiritual development.

*I have to attend to keeping doubt and fear from getting in the way of my happiness and development. What gets in your way, and how do you get past what could hinder you?*

The kind of calling that I have requires so much running, so much traveling and so much intense interaction with larger publics. This goes hand in hand with a certain loneliness in the depths of the soul. You have to take time to cultivate relationships. And when you're on the kind of schedule I'm on, it's very difficult to do that. And so I have to ask myself if I have a fear of wanting to take more time to cultivate a relationship or to reprioritize some of my life. Or is it easier for me to just stay on this intense schedule, and then think that somehow I'm going to succeed in a relationship?

*And how do you answer that question?*

I think I know it in my head, but the question is, can I enact it in my own heart and soul and in my practice? Because as I get older, my schedule tends to intensify. I have two children, so I've already had my chances in a certain sense. My son, Cliff, is 28 and my little daughter, Zeta, is five. Talk about joy—that's as deep as it gets. I've got to make them the priority, no matter what, and give them some idea of what it's like to be deeply loved, so they are cultivating the capacity to love others deeply as they make their journey.

*What kind of relationship would you like to see your son, Cliff, have?*

Well, I don't want him to emulate me. I want him to find himself and be himself. But most of all I want him to be mature, to have a highly cultivated capacity to love, to be patient, to open himself and be vulnerable.

And the same is true when my little daughter matures. She's got to be willing and able to deal with the patriarchal ego and wounded pride of our men; and she still has to keep track of male humanity in such a way that she's open to it, even as she deals with some of the scars that sadly will come just from being a woman in a patriarchal world.

*Black children will continue to catch hell as long as we don't partner better or love each other better. And until building healthy relationships becomes a priority, we won't be able to handle the challenges undermining our progress.*

We should always link any talk about Black love to the struggle for freedom

and courage enacted. Black people have taught the world how to lament in the spiritual. We have taught the world how to deal with darkness and still smile. With our funk we taught the world how to boogie down and shake—even under Jim Crow. But we also need to learn to love each other.

***It's the most revolutionary thing we can do.***

Yes, how we relate to one another is a deeply spiritual issue. And it is the key to our transformation.

# a love supreme, with Alice Coltrane

Not long before she passed away in January 2007, I spent time with Alice Coltrane, master musician, master healer, in a space she had created for all of us. I sat with her at the ashram, truly another world, an abode in the rolling hills of Agoura, California, 40 minutes north of Los Angeles.

A clear-water creek meandered there among massive oaks, refreshing the land and inner landscape of that serenely beautiful sister some called Swamini. Most knew her the way I did, as the wife of the great saxophonist John Coltrane. But as much as she was that, she was so very much more. "I love these trees," I told her, feeling their presence on that day as keenly as I sensed hers—abiding, deeply rooted, always reaching for the light.

For years I had been curious to know how this woman, who grew up in the Baptist Church in Detroit, had come to found an ashram, Sai Anantam, her secluded spiritual retreat where some thirty people live, and another fifty come to nourish their spirit. I wanted to visit and speak with Sister Alice about her spiritual life and her beloved husband, John, who died in 1967.

It seemed strange to write of John Coltrane in the past tense when his spirit remains a vital presence to so many. "John Coltrane lives!" my husband, Khephra Burns, wrote in liner notes for the album *Tribute to John Coltrane*. "Lives! . . . in the courage of artists standing naked before the world, as Coltrane stood, baring his soul for Love's sake, clothed only in the cry of the preacher, the prophet, the mystic." John's death from liver cancer in 1967 left Alice with a daughter, Michelle, from a previous union, and sons John, Jr., who died in an automobile accident at 17; Ravi, a tenor and soprano saxophonist; and Oran, who plays guitar and alto sax. Alice Coltrane—composer,

ALL ABOUT LOVE

246

pianist, organist, harpist—had been off the scene for 26 years when she released *Translinear Light* in 2005. In the interim she founded the ashram in a San Francisco storefront, moving to Agoura in 1982. It was here that I spent a night and a glorious day with the gifted healer and teacher.

*What are your core spiritual beliefs here at the ashram?*
I believe that meditation is the highest spiritual practice, the pathway to God. Our studies of various religions take us a distance. Great lectures by revered, saintly souls may take us even further. However, to know God as Spirit, as consciousness, as truth, we have to engage ourselves so that we can experience the omnipresent God in everything. Meditation to me is the way.

*What is it about the meditative state that allows us to know God's presence?*
The mind is always busy. Even when we are not speaking, the mind is active-thinking, planning, worrying, deducing, rationalizing, speculating. The mind is a great gift, but it has to be quieted down in order to feel, hear and see the presence of God. Meditation is not a philosophical or intellectual pursuit. It is spiritual. When you quiet your mind, you can enter a world of clarity, peace and understanding.

*This ashram is a place of peace. But how do we, who aren't living in so idyllic a spot, stay peaceful in the face of so many competing personal pressures, with our hearts hurting for our neglected community and our children?*
If we are worldly oriented or adversely affected by life's challenges, we cannot give the children the time, attention and guidance they need. But we can receive healing and direction from meditation itself. You don't have to adopt an Eastern religion. You just need to set aside 15 minutes a day to be still. Keep

a little notebook near you to record your experiences. You are going to find there is something in those notes that you require in your life, your family, your work, on your spiritual path. Just as it is fire's nature to burn, it is meditation's nature to heal, to bring peace and uplift you beyond your worldly environment and transport you to a higher plane.

*What is your chosen path, your religion?*
Mine is a Vedic, Eastern path. The name comes from the Vedas, the world's oldest known scriptures proclaimed as emanations from God and compiled during meditation into Four Testaments by the saints and rishis, or holy men. The rishis would write on stone or palm leaves to keep a record of the spiritual renderings and transmissions, and then impart them to the people.

*Were you leaning toward Eastern philosophy and religion before you met John?*
Not at all. John was already interested in Eastern philosophy. Even though his family was Christian, he studied various other faiths, everything from metaphysics, Kabbalah, Hindu mysticism, Sufism, Buddhism, Islam and Judaism to numerology and astrology. In the early sixties John was very much interested in meditation and in the different ways people throughout the world honor God.

*When and how did you two meet?*
It was at Birdland in New York City, in 1963. I played piano with the Terry Gibbs band, and the John Coltrane Quartet was the headliner. Backstage there was a small seating area for musicians. John would always be sitting at the farthest end, and I would take my seat at the opposite end. He had a pensive, contemplative aura, such a quietness and peace about him that I didn't speak to him because I didn't want to disrupt this peace.

After about three days we did speak, and I was highly impressed by his calm manner, his beautiful hands, his serene face, eyes and smile, and his soft, gentle voice. I felt wonderful. It was a joy to converse with him. He talked about music, art, architecture, science in terms of Einstein's theory of relativity, yoga, vegetarianism and so much more.

**How did the romance begin? Did you open your hearts to each other immediately?**
Absolutely! It was a different day, a new day in our lives. Some years later I recall his saying, "Years ago, I had dreamed of you, not knowing that someday we would meet." I will never forget one particular moment backstage. I was walking down the corridor and totally unbeknownst to me John was following me with his horn, and he began playing "Always." That was John's tender and charismatic way of expressing his thoughts through song.

**My husband, Khephra, says when he first heard Meditations he cried. What do you think John was saying through his music?**
He was saying, "Dedicate your life to God, for all is with God." He'd had a spiritual experience and this pointed all of his musical endeavors toward *A Love Supreme*. And despite his receiving accolades from peers, prestigious awards, a Grammy and worldwide acclaim, John dedicated himself completely to God through such albums as *Om* and *Meditations*, and songs like "Dear Lord," "Offering," "Peace on Earth," "Song of Praise" and so many other spiritual compositions.

**Although John was already revered as a pioneer in artistic expression and improvisation, some jazz critics blamed you for the change in his music, saying you led him toward the avant-garde and caused the breakup of the famous John Coltrane Quartet.**

I didn't have to inspire John toward the avant-garde. He led the way on his own. The man was a genius; he didn't need anything from me. That's why it's so interesting that critics decided to dislike me. At some point the members of the quartet felt it was time for a change, and they left on their own. When John said he wanted me to play with him, on piano, I told him there were many others who were qualified. He said, "I want you there because you can do it."

**You were a child prodigy, and John surely appreciated your mastery as a pianist.**
John and I did have a wonderful time making music together. We'd sit at the piano and go through Stravinsky and Schoenberg and Copland, and the children would be around us running and playing.

**John Coltrane the musician, we know. But what was he like as a husband and father?**
He was an excellent husband and father and an obedient son to his mother, who lived in Philadelphia. We lived on Long Island, New York, and he loved to be at home. We always had dinner together and spent a lot of time outdoors taking pictures of our children, watching them play and grow. We were so close; he was so very gentle with us. John never once raised his voice at me or the children. He was at peace with himself and didn't feel he had to use anger to express his feelings. He was fulfilled in his mission in life.

**When John passed away, you were not yet thirty and had four young children. How did you cope?**
In terms of the children, it was very difficult for me. They couldn't understand why their dad did not come home from the studio. Mercifully, God brought me through those hard times. And in some sense, God had prepared me.

Once, prior to John's transition when I was meditating, I saw him walk up to me and say, "I have something to tell you of great importance. I am going." I asked, "Where are you going?" And he said, "I'm going on to enlightenment."

**Did he know he had liver cancer?**
No, I believe that he knew he was quite ill, but I had to practically take him to the doctor for an examination. When his condition was discovered, the doctors said that they needed one more test to fully evaluate the situation. However, he passed on before the final test was taken.

**Were there symptoms?**
He was in pain, very tired, debilitated. Then he told me, "I cannot play my horn anymore." I was shocked. I was speechless.

**I read that you've taken the vow of celibacy.**
Yes, I have vowed celibacy since the time John departed the world. I could not envision myself with someone else. Family members told me, "Give yourself some time." I said no. There is no one who can stand in his place, not even in his shadow.

**What are your days like?**
I live very simply. I'm awake at 4:00 A.M. for meditation. I like to walk around our grounds in the early morning. I take a light breakfast and a normal evening meal around five o'clock. Then I have the rest of the evening to myself, to read, to listen to music, or to spend time with family members or help the grandchildren with their homework. During the day I attend to the evangelical duties and needs of our spiritual organization. I also oversee the

business of our family and Jowcol Music, John's publishing company. It controls all his songs, and there are always requests to use his music in recordings, films, videos.

*Why did you retreat from the jazz world and stay off the scene for twenty-six years?*
After fulfilling my Warner Bros. contract, I really wanted to go deeper into what the Lord had outlined for me to do. I felt that it was time for the next generation of musicians. And the music was changing, so I thought maybe my time was finished.

*This is another existence out here on The Land, as you call it. Music, meditation, chanting, people of all races and backgrounds living in isolation. We think of folks living like this as having dropped out of society.*
These aren't people who don't want to think for themselves. The young people here aren't helpless ones depending on me. They work in the outside world at banks, airlines, accounting firms, schools, doctors' offices. There are many professionals here, people with various college degrees, physical therapists, yoga and special-education teachers. The children go to public schools. We all still have to face our personal tests and our trials in life. This is not a commune. No one was proselytized to come here or solicited in any way. This is an ashram, a place for spiritual refuge where you develop yourself devotionally and spiritually.

*What do you offer residents and initiates? And what do you ask of them?*
I ask that they be sincere in their purpose. We're here for the Lord, and everyone understands and participates in our devotional activities. Meditation, prayer, recitation of the holy names of God, singing the Lord's glories, service

to the community—taking clothing and food to homeless shelters, helping Native American communities, singing to the elders in hospitals, providing them day care and medicine, offering service wherever it's needed. These are the reasons for being here. When we serve humanity, we serve God. What I try to give is the guidance that people might not otherwise have been able to find. Someone may be having difficulty meditating or may be struggling at work, with a child or in a relationship. I offer my inner understanding. God has healed so many people of disorders and diseases here.

### Why an ashram?
I felt this was the next step the Lord ordered me to take.

### Sister Alice, what would you say to Black women? What must we do to find our way home again?
Go within. God is working on the inside. Just go into the sanctuary of your heart, offer your prayers and your worship there. Offer your tears of devotion to the Lord there. God will never, ever fail you. He will receive you.

# notes

ADINKRA SYMBOLS
West African in origin, Adinkra symbols can be
traced back to the seventeenth century.
They were created by the Akan peoples
of Ghana and Côte d'Ivoire
and stamped onto fabric to express the values
and sentiments of the people.
The two symbols below are used throughout the book.

**NYAME NTI**
**by God's grace**

The symbol of faith and trust in God.

**SANKOFA**
**return and get it**

One of the symbols for the importance of learning from the past.

# notes

# notes

# notes

# notes

# notes

# notes

# notes

# notes

# notes

# notes

# notes